SUBMARINE C

MAXIM'S OF PARIS HAS NOTHING ON THE DELICIOUS FOOD SERVED IN AMERICAN SUBMARINES. THE NAVY'S BEST CHEFS BRING YOU THEIR SECRET RECIPES REFINED OVER MANY YEARS UNDER THE SEA.

Why do American submarine sailors universally sing the praises of the food they eat while defending their country? Let the chefs tell you their best tricks and techniques in preparing sumptuous submarine foods.

Submarine Research Center
US NAVAL SUBMARINE BASE, BANGOR
WASHINGTON

SUBMARINE CUISINE

SUBMARINE CUISINE

The secrets of the submarine cooks who, during the past fifty years, have served the best food in the world.

Copyright © 2004, Submarine Research Center

Second edition copyright 2020 published with the express permission of the author. All rights reserved. No part of this publication may be reproduced, stored in a retrieval system or transmitted in any form or by any means, electronic, mechanical, photocopying, recording or otherwise, without the prior written permission of the copyright owner.

Submarine Research Center
ISBN 9798647744340

Forward

Since I was a boy, I have always been fascinated by the submarine. From Jules Verne's *20,000 Leagues under the Sea* to modern movies of submarine warfare, I thrilled to the exploits of these remarkable ships and the brave crews who operate them.

Another long-held passion of mine is cooking. My parents could never figure out where this interest came from. It could be the cooking gene was passed down from a forbearer of mine who I'm told was a cook in the Austro-Hungarian army during the First World War.

Like many amateur chefs, I have a large library of cookbooks, and when I learned of Edward Monroe-Jones' book *Submarine Cuisine,* I was very keen to add a copy to my collection. To my disappointment, I found the book was out of print. Happily, I was able to get in touch with Mr. Monroe-Jones, and he graciously gave his permission to re-publish this fine book.

Anyone who has been aboard a submarine knows the impossibly small dimensions of the submarine galley. How submarine cooks can possibly serve three delicious meals a day to crews of eighty men or more is truly a marvel of organization and ingenuity.

America owes a debt of gratitude to the men and (as of 2011) women who protect and serve their country in the ocean depths around the globe. It is an honor and a privilege to have this small role in sharing a delicious part of their story.

Bon apetit!

Robert Brown
Publisher, *Submarine Cuisine*

INTRODUCTION

When an old submariner remembers his time when the boats were his home he recollects the good times in preference to the moments of stress. The monotony and boredom of so many hours standing watch are mostly forgotten. It is the crew's mess, the conversations, the shipmates and the good humor that stands out in his mind.

This publication has been designed to bring back some of those memories while defining the specifics of submarine food service during the past fifty years. It is a comparative analysis of what exists today in submarine food service and what existed during the Second World War and Cold War. Departing from the academics of the comparison are over fifty recipes reflecting submarine food from 1920 to the present. The volume is intended to be light hearted, and so many humorous incidents are related within the text.

Most of all, it is a nostalgic journey back to the food in the crew's mess around which so many of the good times revolved. Presented in the following pages are descriptions of the problems, frustrations and triumphs of those submarine cooks who dedicated themselves to putting out the best chow possible in conditions that were nearly always a lot less than optimal. Interspersed between these descriptions are the recipes used by submarine cooks. They are authentic submarine recipes, the exact dishes eaten in the crew's mess over a period of about sixty years from S boats, fleet type submarines, Guppies, early nuclear boats and modern fleet ballistic missile submarines. The original recipes were portioned for one hundred men and came from early Navy cookbooks, the Standard Navy Recipe Service, and finally the computerized version found on modern submarines. These recipes have been submitted to retired submarine cooks and other submariner rates for conversion to family size meals. Readers of this publication can now recreate in their kitchens the very same dishes eaten in the after battery of their submarines.

Submarine Research Center started the Submarine Cuisine project by acquiring original cookbooks and recipe cards from retired submarine cooks scattered across the country. A few of them had the foresight to abscond with a set of the cards or book before leaving the Navy. SRC finally was able to find an original 1920 Navy cook book held at the Naval Undersea Museum in Keyport Washington, 1938 and 1944 versions of the improved Navy Cookbook used during the Second World War, a 1953 edition of the Submarine Supplement to the Standard Navy Recipes and a full set of Standard Navy Recipe cards from the 1960s. In the course of these acquisitions many interested participants gave or lent SRC pictures, menus, forms and ancillary books kept by submarine cooks through these many years.

Since not all recipes could be included in this publication it was necessary to produce and distribute to retired submarine cooks a questionnaire, which was intended to reveal the crews' favorite meals, the crews' least liked meals and insights into what it was like to be a submarine cook. The resulting information was collected from forty-two retired cooks and forms the basis for much of the descriptions in Submarine Cuisine.

A passing note on the use of the English language is deserved. The verbs in all description chapters except chapter one dealing with modern submarines are in the past tense. The use of these past tense predicates should not imply that what existed ten, twenty, or fifty years ago does not exist now. The problems of the submarine cook have remained largely the same in spite of technical and space improvements.

To gain an understanding of food service in a modern nuclear submarine SRC interviewed submarine cooks stationed on the Submarine Base at Bangor, Washington and spent portions of two days aboard the USS Alabama (SSBN-731) observing meal preparation and service while in port.

The acknowledgments section recognizes those participants in this project who have generously and graciously given of their time and energy in the completion of questionnaires and the preparation of dishes in their homes. Without the help of so many retired submariners this volume would not have been possible. Of particular importance is the cooperation given by the national office of the USSVI. It was invaluable in the location of retired submarine cooks.

Many individuals having computers responded to SRC's request for help, and, in so far as possible, those contributors have been recognized in the acknowledgments section. It is more than possible that some names have been overlooked or the identity of the participant was not given. SRC apologizes for any oversights and wishes to express its appreciation to all those who helped in this project whether or not their names are listed in the acknowledgments section.

Submarine Research Center solicits readers' comments on the recipes. Its address, email address and telephone number are listed in the title page so that additional printings may carry those comments.

Good reading and good eating.

TABLE OF CONTENTS

	Introduction	5
	Table of Contents	7
	List of Recipes	9
	Acknowledgements	11
1.	Food Service in Today's Submarines	17
2.	Changes in Submarine Food Service Organization	21
3.	Can't-Do-Without Sauces	25
4.	The Place of the Cook in Submarine Organization	29
5.	Famous Submarine Breakfasts	33
6.	What It Was Like To Be a Submarine Cook	39
7.	Favorite Beef Dishes	43
8.	The Standard Navy Recipe Service	53
9.	Three Pork and Ham Dishes	57
10.	Food Storage Aboard Submarines	61
11.	Chicken, a Never-ending Favorite	65
12.	The Evolution of Commissary Record Keeping	73
13.	Regional and Foreign Dishes	91
14.	Popularity Versus Waste	97
15.	A Single Fish Dish	101
16.	Table Etiquette	103
17.	Two Non-meat Entrées	107
18.	The Crew's Favorite Foods	111

19.	Off-beat Salads that Crews Liked	131
20.	Special Dishes and Special Meals	139
21.	Time- The Cook's Master	143
22.	Hearty Soups for In-between Meals	147
23.	The Menu	155
24.	Favorite Desserts	161
25	Baking in a Submarine	174
26	Patrol Reports	179

LIST OF RECIPES

Tomato Sauce	O-20	26
White Sauce	O-1	27
Barbecue Sauce	O-2	28
Creamed Eggs	F-15	34
Minced Beef in Tomato Sauce (SOS)	J-43	35
Dried Beef in White Sauce	J-32	36
Alternate Minced Beef	J-43 and J-32	37
Grilled Hamburgers	J-39	43
Braised Beef	J-9	46
Roast Beef	J-4	47
Ginger Pot Roast	J-11	48
Gravied Beef on Rice		49
Corned Beef and Cabbage	J-26	50
Chicken Fried Steak		51
Baked Virginia Ham	J-77	58
Barbecued Pot Roast of Pork	J-88	59
Kidney Beans, Macaroni with Ham	J-76	60
Creamed Chicken	L-1	66
Roast Chicken	L-5, L-22	67
Bread Dressing to accompany Roast Chicken		68
Fried Chicken, Maryland Style	L-2	69
Barbecued Chicken, Southern Style	L-6	70
Chicken Pot Pie	L-16	71
Brunswick Stew	L-12	72
Chili Con Carne	J-30	92
Shrimp Egg Foo Yong		93
Hawaiian Spare Ribs		94
Teriyaki Steak		96
Salmon Croquettes	H-10	102
Navy Baked Beans	Q-8	108
Corn Fritters	Q-22	109
Macaroni Salad	M-22	132
Cole Slaw	M-16	133
Cottage Cheese Salad	M-41	134
Chicken Salad	M-39	135
Deviled Eggs	F-10	136
Potato Salad	M-26	137
Bean Soup with Hamburger	P-23	148
Hamburger Soup		149
Beef Stew	J-19	150
Baked Bean Soup	J-9	152
Submarine Soup Down		153
Navy Bean Soup	P-23	154

Coffee Cake	C-29	162
Streusel Topping for Coffee Cake		164
Cinnamon Sugar Mix for Coffee Cake		164
Pie Crust	K-1	165
Cherry Pie	K-18	166
Pumpkin Pie	K-34	167
Sweet Potato and Pumpkin Pie		168
Baked Apples	G-19	169
Bread Pudding	G-2	170
Creamy Rice Pudding	G-11	172
Vanilla Cream Pudding	G-18	173

ACKNOWLEGEMENTS AND COMMENTS

Dwayne Larkee, MS1, Roger Nicholson, Daniel Montford and David Holmes, Culinary Specialists, 2nd class (SS) assisted the study by carefully describing the system of food acquisition, storage, retrieval, preparation, service, and waste disposal in Trident boats.

The officers and crew of the USS Alabama (SSBN-731) and in particular, its commanding officer, Melvin Lee, its supply officer, Peter Holdorf and its chief culinary specialist Timothy Pickard.

Submarine Research Center acknowledges the efforts of those retired submarine cooks who completed the SRC questionnaire. They together with some of their comments are as follows:

Norm McKitrick - Raton (SS-270)

Charles Andricci - Ronquil (SS-396), Permit (SSN 594)

Howard Smay - S-23, S-45, S-47, Pampanito (SS-383), Segundo (SS-398), Capitaine (SS-336), Catfish (SS-339), Blower (SS-325) and Pomodon (SS-486).

James Thompson - Hardhead (SS-365), Archerfish (SSN-678).
"When the boats were loading out for an extended run the lead cook used a rule of thumb that required loading for one hundred twenty days at sea regardless of the expected duration."

Julian Powell - Chivo (SS 341), Sea Lion (SS-315), Cavalla (SSK 244), Sam Houston (SSBN-609).

Gerald Pikkart - Sablefish (SS-303), Atule (SS-403).
"The quality of food was excellent irrespective of the length of patrol."

Sam Palmer - Sea Leopard (SS-483), Sirago (SS-485)
"It was a wonderful ride. I would not take the world for the experience. Cab drivers would ask what that smell was. Flowers would let the dogs near them, but not a submariner. Even my wife made me undress on the back porch."

John Franklin - Charr (SS-325), Bugara (SS331), Seadragon (SSN-584), Tirante (SS-420).

John Appleman - Jallao (SS-368).

Richard Gelb - Entemedor (SS-340).

David Lorm - Diodon (SS 349).

Jim Gunter - Quillback (SS-424), Grenadier (SS 525).
"Wouldn't take a million dollars for the experience, but wouldn't give a nickel to do it again. Extremely proud to have served on the boats. Absolutely the best outfit. Some of the best people you will ever meet. They could be depended upon to go the extra mile for a shipmate."

Carroll Dividson - Tinosa (SS-283), Bluegill (SSK242), Sea Fox (SS-402), George Washington (SSBN-598)

James Mayo - Tunny (SSG-282), Barb (SSN 596), Torsk (SS-423), Sirago (SS-485)

Floyd Davis - Hawkbill (SSN-666).

Bob Gregg - Queenfish (SS-393).

Frank Dostal - Diodon (SS-349), Wahoo (SS-565), Halibut (SSN-587).
"Halibut had a galley that was well designed."

William Reighter - Blenny (SS-324).

Art Hoyt - Bergall (SS-320), Bugara (SS-331)
"It was the best time of my life."

Orval Johnston - Stickleback (SS-415), Sabalo (SS-302), Sea Fox (SS-402).

John Smetana - Argonaut (SS-475), Torsk (SS-423), Threadfin (SS-410)
"I am proud to have been designated "Qualified in Submarines"."

George Conro - Queenfish (SS-393), Bream (SS-243), Razorback (SS-394).

Charles Brown- Puffer (SS-268), Bowfin (SS-287), Razorback (SS-394).

Warren Rucker - Grampus (SS 523)

Frederick Cockran - Sterlet (SS 392), Benjamin Franklin (SSBN 640).
"No matter how extravagant the food I served on Sterlet, I could not spend all the money the Navy gave to submarines."

Charles Butler - Becuna (SS-319)
"I made many valuable friends in submarines."

Harold Mulnix - Sturgeon (SS-187)

Edward Gaulrapp - Pompano (SS-491), Runner (SS-476), Odax (SS-484), Requin (SS-481).

Francis Payeur - Sablefish (SS- 303), Sea Owl (SS-405)
"Once a month, when in port I served live Maine lobsters."

Gregory Leonard - Bugara (SS-331), Greenfish (SS-351), Razorback (SS-394).
"I enjoyed the good times and have forgotten the bad times. I would do it all over again in a heartbeat."

Charles Collins - Piper (SS-409)

Richard Smiskol- Trigger (SS-564).
"Those were the good days of my life, aboard the Trigger."

Ivan Witham - Argonaut (SS-475), Tang (SS-563)
"It was tough trying to cheer up the engineers who fought the pancake engines that broke down every three days."

William Benzick - Tunny (SSG-282), Medregal (SS-480), Lizardfish (SS-373)
"The submarine service gave me the best years of my life. It prepared me to take pride in my career and in my life. I gained many life-long friends."

Henry Nielsen - Sea Fox (SS-402), Perch (ASSP-313).
"It was a great period of time to serve as a sea cook. I loved working in attack plot party during general quarters. Loved baking hot rolls for the men going on the four to eight watch."

Kenneth Bambaniti - Corporal (SS-346), LaFayette (SSBN-616).

Pat Lyon - Rasher (SS-269), Jallao (SS-368), Skate (SSN- 578).

William Andersen - Blenny (SS-324), Abraham Lincoln (SSBN-602)
"On the Lincoln I was the baker and loved it. We had pretty much an open galley. I wish I could go back for one more cruise."

James Cooney - Rasher (SS-269), Caiman (SS-323), Sculpin (SSN-590). "I found that I could keep the boys happy with fresh baked goods in the morning. And I always had a pot of good hot soup. I stand six feet four so I never got much guff. My days on the boats were my best."

Ernest Dotter - Sea Dog (SS-402), Becuna (SS-319), Lewis and Clark (SSBN-644).

Several retired submariners forwarded to SRC some of the documents and pictures that had rested in their personal archives for many years. These generous folks include:

Edward F. Gaulrapp
Norma Thomas (wife of the late Chief Thomas)
James Burke
Orval "Casey" Johnston
Frederick E. Cochran
Gerry Patten
William Reighter
Richard Weber
Charles Andricci
Joe Birkle
Philip Beals
Art Salmon

Submarine Research Center appreciates the contributions of Wendy Gulley, Archivist of the Submarine Force Archives in New London, Connecticut. It also wishes to thank Barbara Moe, Archivist of the U.S. Naval Undersea Museum in Keyport, Washington for contributions of early submarine cookbooks.

Those who contributed time and effort in the preparation of the submarine recipes reconstructed for family use deserve special recognition for their willingness to experiment with the Standard Navy Recipes until the product replicated that served on the boats. Most of the participants were retired submarine cooks, but many were not, and it is to the credit of those rates other than cooks that their recipes are so outstanding. Those contributing recipes included:

        Philip Griffith
        James R. Bauman
        Michael LaRose
        Ken Lee
        George and Lynn Lockwood
        Al Caddy
        Warren Hughes
        Lin Marvil
        Rev. Aaron Peters
        William Bentley
        John Franklin
        James Mayo
        Julian Powell
        Howard and Vi Smay
        Jimmy Gunter
        Sam and Betty Palmer
        Richard Gelb
        Joseph Birkle

Thomas Hopely
Charles McGuckin
Nick Louque
Howard Dachs
Frank Dostal
James Thompson
William Benzick
Orval Johnston
John Appleman
Charles Brown
Nickolas Dirkx
James Tierney
George Levitt
Fairman Bockhorst

CHAPTER 1
FOOD SERVICE IN TODAY'S SUBMARINES

Each Trident submarine has a supply officer that has staff rather than line responsibilities. The supply officer is expert in his field of supply and his thorough knowledge of the Navy's supply system renders the commissary department of a modern Trident submarine efficient and effective. The watches he may stand at sea are not central to his job. He is not qualified as nuclear and doesn't stand officer of the deck watches, however, he normally stands diving watches. Submarine supply officers have control over the boats' commissary and supply functions.

The submarine has a committee of enlisted men called the Menu Review Board. This is an advisory panel of petty officers who serve to represent the desires of the crew. Members give suggestions to the lead culinary specialist and supply officer pertaining to menu planning and special events. Where in the past the advisory function was informal and under the responsibilities of the chief of the boat, the Board acts as a conduit between crew and cooks.

The Navy does little warehousing of food. These were abolished in about 1993. It uses wholesale vendors called prime vendors. In the Northwest this means Sysco Corporation. In the Southeast it is the King's Bay System. Food is delivered on a schedule. Normally, food is delivered seventy-two hours after an electronic order has been placed.

Where as in the past most food was distributed from supply points, which were mini-warehouses (such as submarine tenders), the Navy now depends on Just-In-Time delivery systems that are civilian contracted. Many of the concepts within the modern management practice called Total Quality Management have been adopted by the Navy and applied to its food service program.

The food service rates have changed over the years. What were originally cooks became commissarymen, then mess specialists and now the rate is called culinary specialist. A submarine culinary specialist (cook) has as his primary tool in record-keeping the personal computer. It has stored within its hard drive the entire food service organization for the respective submarine. The basic program is supplied by the Navy, but each lead culinary specialist (usually a chief petty officer) has discretion to modify the program to suit the particular needs of the boat. The required forms for budgeting and accounting are kept and submitted by email. Menus and inventory are maintained on computer.

Enlisted men receive an allowance for food as a part of their pay. The allowance is then given to the boat. If the person has not given the commuted rations (comrat) over to the boat he must pay for each meal eaten, just as officers do.

A computer inventory consists of what exists, what has been consumed (meals consumed and stores used is from a hand edited form). Also on the computer form is the amount of income, i.e., base allowance per man plus various special categories which total about $7.80 per day per man, (2004). The amount allowed a submarine per day is calculated for the crew irrespective of how many may actually eat. While in port the boat will accumulate money which may be used for more extravagant meals when the boat goes to sea.

Menus are prepared over a five week period. They are on computer under a nutritional program that provides variety, taste, appearance and nutrition. The menu is approved by the Board, supply officer and captain. Posted menus are replaced each week.

In fast attack submarines food is brought aboard much as it has always been: brought to the pier in trucks, then hand carried into a submarine through vertical hatches. In Trident submarines food is brought in modules (a container approx. six feet by six feet by five feet) They are aluminum containers, similar to a civilian aircraft cargo container. The module is lowered into the boat by crane. The escape trunk is removed providing an abnormally large opening (about twelve feet in diameter) into the pressure hull. After the module has been lowered into the boat it is power-dollied into a storage position. Each container is stored in such a way that food is accessible as it is to be used meal by meal. The ordering submarine has specified the menu schedule and computers have produced a loading diagram that allows for sequential food access. When the containers are brought aboard, the added weight is reported to the engineer who compensates the boat accordingly.

The submarine's design incorporates dedicated spaces to exactly accommodate the food containers. The fleet ballistic missile submarine does not experience severe space problems as had predecessor boats. Fast attack submarines do not share this luxury and in spite of having much more space than diesel boats, must rely upon many of the old techniques of catch-as-catch-can storage.

Culinary specialists have the authority to deal directly with retail vendors if they wish. In such case the culinary specialist will complete an 1149 form. This is an open purchase document. Representatives of the specialty food product meets with the ship's lead culinary specialist and makes a preliminary sale. Then the order is electronically placed with the vendor (Sysco, King's Bay or other) which will buy the product from the specialty house and will deliver it on a schedule determined by the submarine. The turn around time on special orders is about two weeks.

It is possible to provide special foods on submarines for special purposes. When carrying Marines the boat may order special foods from the authorized vendor and will have a special allowance above the base amount for this purpose.

The leading culinary specialist keeps track of the allowance and expenditures. He is responsible for not over-expending. The mess is run on a monthly basis. Reports are electronically submitted monthly to Washington DC. The computer relieves the specialist of the tedious arithmetic that burdened cooks in years past.

The captain's influence on the menu and types of foods served is probably more apparent on modern submarines than in past years. This is a product of the Navy's interest in physical fitness. For example, a captain may want low fat foods or have a dislike for certain foods. He may be interested in keeping hydrocarbons out of the boat's atmosphere and so may limit the amount of fried foods or the use of deep fat fryers. He signs all menus.

Limitations on smoking are up to each captain, however, every boat limits smoking to either one space, (fast attacks) or two spaces, (Tridents). During drills and battle stations smoking is not allowed. Men line up to use the smoking space (which accommodates normally about three men) after a drill or after battle stations have been secured. Smoking is never allowed in the crew's mess.

Three formal meals are served each day. It takes about one and one half hours to prepare a meal and to set up for it. Most meals are buffet style. In a Trident boat a steam tray houses the hot items and an ice tray the chilled items, normally a salad bar. Men line up, serve themselves and sit down to eat. There are normally three sections: the relieving section, the off-going section and the fill-in section. In fast attack boats the men serve themselves cafeteria style for certain items and sit at tables where the entrée and other items are served on platters by mess cooks

While at sea breakfast is served from five AM to about six. Lunch is served from eleven AM to about twelve noon. Dinner is served from five PM to about six PM. These short eating schedules reflect the need for crew's mess space for training. The schedule works for all one hundred ninety men as long as each man eats in about fifteen minutes. The crew's mess accommodates about thirty men at a time.

In a typical fleet ballistic missile submarine a chief petty officer will be the leading petty officer in charge of food service. He is responsible for the galley, scullery, crew's mess and food storage spaces. He is responsible also for the acquisition, storage, replenishment, preparation and serving of food. He keeps and supervises the keeping of related records on food purchases, consumption and survey. Under his supervision is a first class petty officer, who is the leading petty officer in the space. This person directly supervises three or four 3rd and 2nd class petty officers. There are normally four mess cooks who are seamen or third class petty officers in rates other than food service.

The Chief will normally stand a watch in control. The first class petty officer runs the mess and galley, keeps the records and supervises others. The second and third class petty officers do the actual cooking and baking.

Advancement in rate requires a great deal of self study and sometimes special schools. The Navy sends deserving culinary specialists to the Culinary Institute of America and the main source of study information comes from a book written by the CIA. Exams are given in March of every year. A man may pass the test, but not make the next higher rate because of a lack of slots. His ultimate standing is determined by a series of factors such as time in rate, score on test, performance evaluations and others. The examination for chief petty officer includes the following rate topics: food safety and equipment, administration, nutrition and menu planning, baking, management, and food production.

It also includes general Navy knowledge including: anti terrorism and force protection, military justice, naval organization, uniforms and first aid. Only a small proportion of those taking and passing the test actually receive promotion to the next higher grade.

Modern submarine cooking tends to emulate civilian cooking standards. Both the types of meals served, the variety of meals and attention to nutrition are the civilian oriented factors. Since the Navy now places emphasis on weight control and physical fitness, food service reflects the commensurate low calorie items.

A Trident submarine recycles its paper and aluminum. Refuse other than garbage is compacted and placed into empty food containers. Each modern submarine has a sophisticated garbage ejector. The garbage ejector can be used down to test depth. Breech door and muzzle door have five separate interlocks. Metal canisters come as a sheet, are folded and a weight is added, normally seven pounds. Garbage is compacted into cylinders that fit into the metal containers. Garbage is ejected on a schedule and requires the approval of the conning officer.

A modern fleet ballistic missile submarine consumes on a typical patrol 4000 pounds of beef, 3000 pounds of sugar, 1200 pounds of coffee, 120 pounds of tea, 2000 pounds of Chicken, 1400 pounds of pork loin, 1000 pounds of ham, 800 pounds of butter, 3400 pounds of flour and 11,520 eggs.

CHAPTER 2
CHANGES IN SUBMARINE FOOD SERVICE ORGANIZATION

It is difficult to define the role of the submarine cook in a generalized setting because that role has changed during the course of submarine development. Before the fleet type submarine had been designed the Navy had relied principally on "O", "R" and "S' class boats. These submarines were, by today's standards, primitive and dangerous.

Being much smaller than the fleet type submarine the early boats of the American Navy had little space for food storage or preparation. It seems as though the designers of the early boats considered food as a secondary necessity of submarine operation. Their failure to provide for adequate food service space was predicated on the limited mission of the early boats. They were considered merely as adjuncts to the main surface fleet and were not intended to stay at sea for prolonged periods. As a result there was only a small space (about the size of a fleet type boat's pantry) devoted to food preparation. They lacked a crew's mess or dedicated eating space. The men ate while sitting on their bunks. The space limitations meant that submarine food tended to be rudimentary in form and taste. The crew gulped their food from bowls and sometimes trays. Seldom did they receive anything other than bare subsistence food.

The German Navy through the Second World War also lacked any real food preparation and serving space. The crew ate at their bunks using bowls and spoons. The standard diet was "Eintopf" which means "one dish". Meats, vegetables and spices were cooked together into a stew-like meal which was served on a catch-as-catch-can basis.

Little thought was given to nutrition in the early American and German boats.

The American fleet type submarine was designed in response to America's need for an ocean going, long range submarine that could endure long patrols across the Pacific. Such a submarine had to attend to the needs of the crew who would man the submarine during operations lasting two or more months. Adequate berthing and food preparation were factored into the early designs. The after battery compartment was devoted to berthing, lavatories, galley, scullery, and a small crew's dinette. The crew's eating space or mess was large enough to accommodate about one third of the crew at a time. This space allocation was predicated on the standard watch rotation bill. The division of time into four-hour watches meant that two thirds of the crew would be off watch and available to eat while one third of the crew was standing watch.

The three sections were thus assigned eating positions in terms of their proximity to the watch. The one-third section of the crew that was about to relieve the watch was fed first. The second-section to be fed was the off watch section. These men ate while the watch was being relieved. The last third of the crew to eat was the relieved section.

This tidy arrangement was a natural division that matched the normal cruising operation of the submarine. It has become so much a part of submarine life that modern nuclear submarines feed their crews in exactly the same manner.

The fleet type submarine had a forward battery compartment. This part of the boat was reserved for the officers. The compartment held only a very small space for food preparation. It was called the pantry and was located just forward of the wardroom, which itself was small. The pantry could accommodate only one person, but it need not be larger since the officers ate the same food as the crew. The pantry was manned by the steward on watch. This person brought food from the galley in the after battery compartment to the pantry where he garnished the food and arranged it on serving platters.

The wardroom itself was a multipurpose space. It sat its approximate seven or eight officers at a table with white tablecloth, napkin rings and cups/saucers. When not in use as a food eating space the wardroom served as a work space for the officers. The white table cloth was removed to expose a green felt cloth upon which sat books, charts and instruments. In times of emergency the wardroom table was used as an operating table where more than one man's life was saved. When the fleet type submarines became Guppies the wardroom served as a combat information center and attack center.

The wardroom also accommodated activities on the lighter side. Officers on long patrols played cards, read books and watched movies. The actual card games played was entirely at the discretion of the commanding officer. If he played bridge and a junior officer did not, it would be in the junior officer's best interest to learn. This could be said of canasta and hearts. Poker was sometimes played in the wardroom, although many skippers forbade any kind of gambling.

The remainder of the forward battery compartment was designed for officers and chief petty officers' berthing. Tucked into the after starboard corner of the compartment was a tiny yeoman's space.

The same training and leisure activities were carried out in the after battery compartment where the men not only ate, but enjoyed themselves between meals. As a matter of fact, it can be said that the crew's mess was the center of the ship's social make-up. A first class petty officer when off watch looked forward to having a cup of coffee in the crew's mess where he could bitch and moan about the Navy and life in general as well as listening to others doing the same thing. A wise captain could listen to the quality of the grousing in the after battery to get a good handle on the morale of the crew. Strangely, the two were directly proportional. That is, the higher the level of grumpy comments about the world in general the higher the morale of the crew. It can be safely said that the crew's mess was not only an eating place, but a vent for the psychological pressures that built up during long patrols.

The crew's mess in a fleet type boat and Guppy was the focal point of social interaction. Movies were shown there once per night while on patrol. Tournaments at cards, acey-deucey and other games were held there and cigarettes were smoked as gallons of coffee were consumed.

Modern fleet ballistic missile submarines are only faintly similar to the fleet type submarine in so far as the informal use of the crew's mess is concerned. The mess area is five to six times larger than that of a fleet type boat and the galley is about the same in terms of expanded capacity. While on a fleet type boat meals were served to the crew via large serving platters that were filled by mess cooks, the modern submarine has gone to a buffet style serving arrangement. Men pick out their food from a variety that is much more diverse than in years past. At the breeze-way between galley and mess, culinary specialists serve the entrée of choice.

This may seem like an improvement, but the men are limited in eating time to fifteen or twenty minutes and then must vacate the mess so that others may sit down. The limitations of food service in modern submarines stem largely from the increased size of the crews.

When one looks over the span of years from the "O" boats in the twenties to the current operational fast attack and missile submarines one can see the improvements that have been made. There is the tendency, however, to look back on the good old days when foul smelling diesel sailors sat around the after battery and enjoyed each other's company. The boats were simpler then and men knew virtually everything about every piece of equipment in the boat. Modern submarines are so complex that specialization has been inevitable. This has lead to natural divisions within the crew. Men of the same rate tend to congregate and discuss the business at hand, but continual social interaction between all crew members is lacking.

A further division has arisen from the technical knowledge and skill required to control the propulsion reactor. Men in the engineering department have limited issues in common with the torpedomen and fire control technicians. The need for security has built invisible walls between some of the technical rates.

The crew's mess is used for training during off-eating hours. Training is essential in the complex operation of the modern submarine. There is little time for leisure. As a result the crew's mess is no longer the center of social interaction. There are other spaces in the modern submarine that compete for this honor.

All this impacts on the submarine culinary specialist and the food that is served on submarines. Clearly, the modern submarine serves a better variety of food, but the operational constraints of these boats render the eating of meals as more mechanical and less social. Throughout it all, over the years one commonality has remained a constant: submarine cooks are proud of their work and the quality of the meals served by them.

CHAPTER 3
CAN'T-DO-WITHOUT SAUCES

French cooking is known for its sauces. Even the most humble of meats and vegetables can be rendered supreme by the quality of the sauce that covers them. What steak cannot be improved by the addition of a delicate Béarnaise sauce? Even the household Worcestershire sauce is used to flavor a variety of dishes in addition to its basic use as a meat taste enhancer. Indeed, it might be said that many meals are made or broken by the quality of the sauce used.

The Navy takes a traditional and conservative approach to sauces. While it encourages limited experimentation it must recognize that a meal for hundreds or even thousands of men represents a considerable investment. It is not about to risk spoiling expensive meats by the injection of unknown flavors. On the other hand, many medium quality meats can be made into flavorful entrees if the right sauce is used.

The Standard Navy Recipe Service has a section devoted to sauces. One subsection deals with dessert sauces, but that is beyond the interest of this study. The remaining subsections attend to two basic sauces and from these all other sauces are derived.

From the basic tomato based sauce (O-20) comes all the sauces for Italian and Mexican dishes. Charles Brown offers his basic tomato sauce. Depending on the added spices one can make sauces for spaghetti, pizza, and Hawaiian dishes. The barbecue sauce is really a derivation of the tomato sauce with additional spices.

The white sauce (O-G-1) can be turned into any number of specialized sauces. Typical additions include celery, cheese, curry, egg, horseradish, mushrooms and onion. Combinations of these together with parsley, peppers, pimiento and crab make many regional dishes. Hollandaise, Mornay and other special sauces all start with a white sauce base.

Most gravies are also derived from a white sauce having the same butter and flour roux. The key to flavorful gravies is to scrape from the pan the meat's leavings and to blend this flavor with the more subtle flavors of butter and flour.

CHARLES BROWN'S TOMATO SAUCE (O-20)

One might reasonably ask why a recipe for tomato sauce should be included in the most-used recipes of the submarine service. Tomato sauce was sort of a catalyst for a number of recipes that made up into styles of spaghetti and other dishes where a tomato base might be needed. Here, Charles Brown not only offers his recipe for the sauce, he adds a quick note so that one might roll out a few meat balls to go with the sauce.

Ingredients	Measure/Weight	Method
Shortening	1 ounce	Melt shortening, add onions
Onions, finely chopped	1/2 onion	and garlic. Sauté for 5 min.
Garlic, chopped	1 small clove	until the onions are browned.
Flour, wheat	Enough to thicken shortening	Blend in flour
Water, hot	1/4 cup	Combine water, tomato puree,
Tomato puree	8 oz.	sugar, salt, pepper, cayenne
Sugar	dash	pepper, cinnamon and cloves
Salt	dash	
Pepper	dash	
Pepper, cayenne	dash	
Cinnamon	dash	
Cloves, ground	dash	Gradually add to onions, stirring constantly. Heat to boiling temperature, reduce heat and simmer 15 minutes, stirring constantly.

A very nice meat sauce can be made by adding ground beef to the sauce.

For meat balls to go with spaghetti accomplish the following:
Mix about a half pound of hamburger with a small amount of minced onion and minced celery, plus one egg. Work this in thoroughly then add 1/4 cup of bread crumbs. Mash contents and roll into small balls. Place on baking tray and do a partial bake at 375 Deg F for 20 minutes. Add to the sauce and finish baking at 375 Deg F for another 30 minutes.

THE NAVY'S BASIC WHITE SAUCE (O-1)

The Standard Navy Recipe for making a basic white sauce is essential to master, because so many recipes start with the sauce. While the recipe calls for large amounts of ingredients that make up gallons of sauce the following will serve to make up enough sauce for a number of dishes that are traditional to the Navy. Minced beef on toast and creamed eggs are two of the most common uses of white sauce. Notice that the roux described in those recipes is a simple mixture of butter and flour with salt and pepper. Added to that is milk in whatever quantity is needed to gain the right consistency.

Ingredients	Measure/Weight	Method
Butter	1/2 stick or 1/8 pound	
Flour	About 3 tbsp	With a fork mash the flour into the butter making a soft but solid ball.
Salt	Pinch	
Pepper	Pinch	Mash the seasoning into the ball and place in a bowl.
Milk	Enough to thin roux	With a wisk mix small amounts of cold milk into the roux. Be sure to mix thoroughly before adding more milk. Continue to add milk in small amounts until the mixture is the desired viscosity.

This is one of those basic recipes that is quickly committed to memory and then repeated many times for various dishes. A good cook masters the tomato sauce recipe and the white sauce recipe at the beginning of his submarine cooking career.

NICK DIRKX'S BARBECUE SAUCE (O-2)

Nick qualified on the Chivo (SS-341) and served as cook on the Bonefish (SS-582), Bream (SS243), Tiru (SS-416) and Nathan Hale (SSBN-623). So many meat entrées depend on a good barbecue sauce that Nick has converted the Standard Navy Recipe for the sauce into a flexible mixture that is good for beef, chicken and pork.

Ingredients	Measure/Weight	Method
Vinegar	1/4 cup + 2 tbsp	
Sauce, Worcestershire	3 tbsp	
Sugar, brown	2 tbsp	Mix vinegar, sauce and sugar.
Tomato sauce	7/8 cup	
Salt	2 and 1/4 tsp	
Mustard, prep.	1 and 1/2 tbsp	
Pepper, Cayenne	1/4 tsp	
Pepper, green finely diced	1 tbsp	
Celery, finely diced	3 tbsp	
Cloves, ground	1/4 tsp	
Allspice	1/4 tsp	
Chili powder	1 tsp	Thoroughly mix ingredients and simmer for 30 to 40 minutes until the ingredients are blended.

This recipe makes up about six portions and can be stored in refrigerator. It is used over roasting meats.

Catsup can be substituted in place of tomato sauce for a slightly spicier taste.

CHAPTER 4
THE PLACE OF THE COOK IN SUBMARINE ORGANIZATION

The captain is responsible for every operation within the submarine including the food served to the men. He, or in his place, the executive officer assigns departmental responsibilities to the officers. On diesel type submarines all officers were line officers and the duty of the commissary department was normally assigned to the most junior of the officers. The commissary department went hand in hand with the supply department and thus an officer recently out of submarine school was normally assigned these departments upon his arrival at his first operating submarine.

Large, modern submarines in the American Navy have both line and staff officers including a staff supply officer who assumes the duties of supply and commissary officer. His training has been exclusively in the area of supply and he comes well equipped to handle the submarine's supply responsibilities. Fleet ballistic missile submarines with large crews that are doubled and known as blue and gold crews also are staffed with medical doctors. Earlier type submarines had only a pharmacist's mate who acted as a doctor.

Those individuals who in some manner controlled the work of the submarine cook included the captain, the commissary officer and to some extent the medical representative, be he a pharmacist's mate or a medical doctor.

Officers eating in the wardroom had no separate food preparation space. Officers ate the same food as the crew with stewards who bring food from the galley to the pantry which lies in close proximity to the wardroom. Here the stewards arranged and garnished the galley-prepared food and served it to officers on trays. The stewards influenced the galley routine to a small extent by having access to it and by occasionally requesting of cooks specially prepared dishes.

Without question the primary customer of the submarine cook was every man in the crew. As is pointed out continuously in this publication, the cook's sole job was to please the crew. On most submarines a happy captain in so far as food preparation was concerned was a captain with a crew that was well fed.

There was in years past a sort of informal perception of rates in a submarine. Cooks suffered from an unjustified stigma of being a less critical rate. Fortunately, this perception has disappeared, partly because the importance of nutrition has taken such an important position in the welfare of the ship and partly because it is recognized that the single limiting factor in a submarine's endurance is food.

The typical fleet type and Guppy submarines had either a chief or first class cook as lead cook and about four other cook petty officers to accomplish the large work load involved in food service. Assisting them were about three mess cooks whose job it was to keep the galley, scullery and mess clean. They prepared salads and refilled the serving bowls as crew members ate their way through the food.

Some seaman assigned to mess cooking liked the work and soon began to take part in meal preparation. If they showed a little zeal and talent they might be given responsibilities that were a little beyond their submarine experience.

For example Rod Nielsen was just a seaman working toward qualification on the Sea Fox (SS-402) in the 1950s when the chief of the boat assigned him mess cooking duties. Although he was a seaman, he had always liked cooking and so talked the chief of the boat, Rod Nuttleman into designating him a cook striker. He started standing watches with the petty officer cooks. All went well with Seaman Nielsen and he developed a quiet air of superiority over the other seamen who stood lookout, planes and helm watches.

Not being qualified he didn't know much about charging batteries and he certainly didn't know that what went on in the maneuvering room had an effect on his duties in the galley. For example he didn't know that when the charge reached the finishing rate the current to his oven increased - not a lot, but enough to throw his timing for roast chicken off. The chicken was hopelessly burned and there was no time for a replacement meal. He tasted one and convinced himself that the burnt flesh was hardly noticeable. Nielsen was on his own and he decided to serve the birds as they were.

Chief Nuttleman spit his first taste out and promptly relieved Nielsen of his striker status. The young submariner resigned himself to becoming one of the seamen standing lookout, planes and helm watches.

Seaman Nielsen was an anomaly among the thousands of young submariners assigned to mess cooking. Most simply accepted the dreary clean-up work for anywhere from a month to three months with the resignation of being the lowest man on the totem pole. The duty was rotated among the least trained in the crew on a schedule normally determined by the chief of the boat. While the mess cooks had to live up to cleanliness standards set by the lead cook and to a lesser extent the doc, they were handicapped by their multiple jobs of learning their rate, qualifying in submarines and carrying out the orders of the cook. It was not uncommon for the on-coming mess cooks to appear in questionable sanitary condition.

A green lieutenant junior grade (Gil) on a Guppy in 1956 had just reported aboard and assumed responsibility for the commissary department in the novel, "Of Wives and Submarines". He observed the following:

"Two mess cooks were getting ready to prepare the salads. Big stainless steel bowls sat on a table with heads of lettuce and tomatoes and onions. Greenwood yelled out from the galley for the two teen aged enginemen to wash their hands. This they dutifully did in the scullery, but Gil noticed that their hands emerged, still with bilge grease under the fingernails and the creases of their palms. Gil watched them with interest, since food preparation was to be one of his responsibilities. After they had cut up the lettuce and thrown it into the bowls, they poured in an abundance of vinegar. They then tossed the salad with their hands. Gilhooly noticed that as the vinegar mixed with the greens, the hands of the enginemen apprentices became sparkling clean.

"Gil discerned that the bilge grease formerly wedged under the finger nails was now clinging to the lettuce leaves. He would have brought this to the attention of the mess cooks, but he noticed that the petty officers who remained seated continued to converse while watching them. Gilhooly concluded that if these men were comfortable with less-than-sanitary salad mixing, far be it for him to discourage a practice that must have preceded him by many years. He reasoned that the Razorback smells got into the men by varied routes, one of which was the salads they ate."

It has been suggested by more than one submarine cook participating in the preparation of this publication that a small bottle of diesel fuel be kept in the kitchen of old submariners. An eye dropper would be excellent for adding a drop of the fuel to many of the dishes described herein. This suggestion has been made in the name of authenticity and is not applicable to nuclear submariners.

It might be arguably said that in an American submarine the senior cook is recognized as being more critical to the mission's success than any other rate in a submarine. This being the case the captain's reliance on the senior cook for maintenance of crew stamina is more direct than it was on fleet type submarines. A common thread running through every submarine command from the Second World War to the present is the respect demanded by the exceptional cook. Captains have always busted a gut to get a really good cook and will do most anything to keep one on board.

During the Second World War a cook's training was mostly on-the -job training. Now it is not uncommon for submarine cooks to attend one the several Culinary Institute of America facilities. These are the most prestigious schools for the culinary arts. One is located in Napa Valley of California and the other is on the Hudson River in New York. The Navy has modern training schools and pride in the culinary arts within the modern submarine Navy is remarkable. Submarine food in today's Navy can truly be called cuisine. While it is true that factors inherent in a submarine sometimes limit the ability of its cooks, there is no doubt that today's submarine cooks can compete with the best chefs in the best restaurants of the country.

This seems to imply that submarine cooks of the fleet type and Guppy boats were less competent. This is not the case. The cooks of fifty years ago worked in an inhospitable environment, often with less than perfect foods and in difficult sea conditions. In spite of these disadvantages the submarine cook served meals that were relished by the men and worthy of praise.

CHAPTER 5
FAMOUS SUBMARINE BREAKFASTS

An examination of submarine menus reveals that most breakfasts were constructed around four basic elements: eggs, cereals, sauces and fruits.

Most sailors enjoyed eggs to order with the usual fixings including bacon, sausage, toast, butter and some form of potato. It should be remembered that in the 1940s and 50s the Navy didn't pay much attention to calories and fat intake. If the average submarine cook served eggs to order every day of the week there would have been little complaint. This was the main-stay of the submarine breakfast both in the forward and after batteries.

"Cereals, assorted" were tumbled onto the tables in the form of little boxes filled with General Mills and Kellogg's varieties. Before these came into being in the early 1950s cereal was in bigger boxes with less choice, but the effect was the same. The men never tired of the cold cereal. Hot cereal was a rarity. It was just too much trouble. The cereal choices were normally in addition to eggs to order.

Creamed minced beef (SOS) in tomato sauce was served over toast at least two or three times a week. This broke up the eggs monotony. It was sometimes served in addition to the eggs, but often represented the main course. This was alternated with Creamed Dried Beef (J-32) also known as chipped beef or Foreskins. The reader of this publication will take note that submariners don't remember the eggs to order, but they are quick to condemn or praise the Navy's two creamed beefs on toast.

Hardly was there a breakfast without "Chilled Fruit" or in the latter stages of a patrol "Chilled fruit juice". Before the advent of frozen- concentrated orange juice and later other juices the liquid was canned and had a simply awful taste. Chilled or not, it wasn't a hit with submariners, but when frozen foods and juices became abundant the breakfast table held pitchers of wholesome juices.

For as long as they lasted, the boats served fresh oranges and grapefruit which were halved and eaten with relish. The shelf life of fresh fruit was amazingly long. It was their bulk that limited their use on a submarine.

MICHAEL LAROSE'S CREAMED EGGS (F-15)

Michael LaRose qualified on the Sea Owl (SS-405) during the late sixties, then served the remaining part of his twenty year hitch on six nuclear powered boats the last of which was the Andrew Jackson (SSBN-619). He was a sonarman and made seventeen special operation tours

The first variation of the Standard Navy Recipe for creamed eggs is called Scotch Woodcock. Where the title comes from is unknown, since Scotch is a drink and the adjective in reference to the country is "Scottish". Both S.O.S. and this version of creamed eggs are served over toast. Judy and Mike have reduced the recipe. It makes into four large servings.

Ingredients	Measure/Weight	Method
Eggs, hard boiled	6 large	After hard boiling the eggs, peel and cut into eighths. Set aside in casserole dish.
Butter	1/4 cup	
Flour, White, sifted	1/4 cup	In a saucepan melt butter over low heat. Gradually add flour to butter stirring constantly with wire wisk until a smooth roux is rendered.
Milk	1 and 3/4 cup	Heat milk to near boiling. Gradually add milk to roux while over low heat, stirring constantly with wisk.
Cheese, shredded, medium cheddar.	2 ounces	Add shredded cheese and stir until melted into sauce. To thicken sauce add more cheese or less milk.
Bread crumbs, buttered	1 tbsp	
Salt	pinch	
Pepper	pinch	Pour sauce over eggs in casserole dish. Sprinkle bread crumbs over sauce. Place casserole dish in pre-heated 325 deg F oven for 20 minutes. Serve over toast.

The original recipe calls for condensed milk, but this makes an overly rich cream. On the submarine a combination of condensed and powdered milk was used, however, for the family, use whole milk.

CHARLES BROWN'S S.O.S. (MINCED BEEF, J-43)

Charles Brown is one of the Second World War submarine cooks who has many stories to tell. He served on several boats including the Bowfin, (SS-287), the Puffer, (SS-268), the Razorback (SS-394), the Pomfret (SS-391) and the Bergall (SS-320). He is probably the most experienced submarine cook that SRC has had the honor to interview. As such, he was awarded the prestigious task of preparing the most celebrated submarine dish - S.O.S.

Charles was enthusiastic about the Submarine Cuisine project and produced more recipes from memory. Several pages are devoted to his talents and remarkable memory of old-time submarine recipes outside of the Standard Navy Recipe Service.

Ingredients	Measure/Weight	Method
Beef, boneless, ground	1/2 pound	Braise beef and onions. Add flour and brown.
Onions, chopped	1 onion	
Flour, wheat	App 2 tbsp	
Shortening	1/2 tsp	Use enough flour to make a roux.
Tomatoes, canned	1 20-oz, can	Add tomatoes, spices, water.
Mace or nutmeg	Pinch	
Salt	Pinch	
Pepper	Pinch	
Water	As needed	Let simmer for 10 to 15 minutes. Stir often.

This heavy beef sauce with tomato essence was typically served over toast for breakfast.

An option was to disguise the recipe by omitting the tomato sauce and mace or nutmeg. Instead of water a beef stock could be used with Worcestershire Sauce. Then by increasing the flour and adding a bit of butter for smoothness the submariners could be served "creamed beef on toast." (This was not Foreskins, the recipe for which appears on the following page.)

CHARLES BROWN'S VERSION OF CREAMED DRIED BEEF (J-32)

The first cousin to S.O.S. was known in the vernacular as Foreskins. Its actual title was creamed dried beef. This was also a breakfast dish and was served over toast as was S.O.S. The basic white sauce was from O-G-1 in the Standard Navy Recipes, however, it was such a basic recipe that all submarine cooks simply worked by instinct. The actual recipe converted to family size by Charles Brown appears as follows:

Ingredients	Measure/Weight	Method
Butter	1/2 stick	
Flour	Enough for roux	Combine the small amount of flour with room temperature butter by mashing with a fork. Add enough flour until the mixture is a thick paste.
Milk	Enough for purpose	Add warm milk to mixture while whipping the paste into a medium white sauce.
Beef, dried, sliced	One small jar	Cut the pieces into bite size. Place in small amount of water and cover. Bring to boil. Let stand for five minutes.
White pepper	Pinch	Add pepper to mixture, add beef to mixture. Stir in thoroughly. Serve over toast.

There was never any agreement among submariners as to which of the two traditional recipes was the more popular. The after battery gripers moaned and groaned when either S.O.S. or Foreskins was served, but it was those same complainers that had several servings of the two recipes. Both are fattening.

WILLIAM BENTLEY'S ALTERNATE MINCED BEEF (J-43 and J-32)

This is an interesting recipe, since it seems to fall halfway between S.O.S. and Foreskins. Notice that the sauce is a white base, but uses a ground beef rather than dried chipped beef. It is Bill Bentley's answer to the never ending argument over which of the two dishes was the most popular.

Ingredients	Measure/Weight	Method
Beef, ground Sausage, chopped	2 cups 1/2 cup	Heat a skillet on high heat. Place the beef and sausage into skillet and brown while stirring with wooden spoon. Transfer the browned meat to a bowl leaving the fat in the skillet.
Milk Flour	2 cups 1/2 cup	Wisk the flour into the fat to make a roux. Add milk and flour in alternate small amounts while on low heat, bringing the contents to a simmer.
Salt Pepper	pinch pinch	Add salt and pepper. Simmer for two minutes while constantly stirring. Stir in the meat and continue to stir.
Eggs	6	Boil and shell the eggs, chop them finely.

Place hot toast or biscuit on warmed plate. Butter the toast or biscuit heavily. Add small amount of shredded sharp cheddar cheese. Ladle enough meat sauce over the toast or biscuit to smother the cheese. Sprinkle liberal amount of chopped egg and a dash of paprika.

This (as well as the other breakfast recipes) should not be subjected to a calorie count. Likewise, fat content should be ignored. In the 1940s and 50s submariners were unaware of such trifles.

CHAPTER 6
WHAT IT WAS LIKE TO BE A SUBMARINE COOK

If the job of submarine cook could be reduced to one word, it would have been pride. No other job on a submarine gave such immediate response to quality of work. When a meal met with the approval of the crew they showed it. When it fell short of expectations they showed that too. Most submarine jobs pertained to machinery. When occasionally equipment failed it got fixed and perhaps an officer would show gratitude for a job well done, but only the cook had immediate feedback three times a day. It may be said that the job of cook was intensely human. Reaction to his work was always a human reaction and his assimilation of the reaction was so human as to be emotional. If ever a person was attached to his work by this human umbilical cord it was the ship's cook.

Of critical importance to the cook's reputation was the quality of his coffee. There's normally not much that can go wrong with coffee, but when something does go wrong it's a real problem for the cook.

K-boats were small and unusual. There was little room for anything and since the mission of the K-boats was sonar picket duty they stayed out longer than their size would comfortably accommodate. The coffee urn was between the galley and crew's mess, but the slot built for it barely allowed room for its top cover to be lifted. This situation was aggravated by the chief cook's storage of cigarette cartons in what little space was above the urn.

Lee Rogers reported that in 1954 after a month at sea the coffee took on a bitter taste that prompted the wrath of the crew. The men groused about the cook's lousy coffee for two weeks until he finally decided to clean the urn. He found a sodden carton of cigarettes in the urn wedged under the filter. The discovery was most helpful in getting at the cause of the men's jittery nerves. The combination of caffeine and nicotine produced some very irritable submariners, but after the urn-cleaning everything got back to normal.

SRC's survey revealed that thirty two percent of submarine cooks believed that the most important factor in their job satisfaction was their contribution to crew morale. Their comments included, "Watching crew members dig into the chow", "Perking up tedious operations", "Being of service to my shipmates" and "Satisfying crew members through my own efforts".

Ranking with equal status (32%) was a cook's receipt of praise from shipmates. Comments included, "Looking at smiling faces", "The words -'Good Chow' at end of a meal" and "Immediate praise".

Other factors in the job satisfaction survey included working with little supervision, pride in knowing that what we did was the best, being in the hub of activity, greeting every crew member every day, and eating my own food.

It is no wonder that each submarine cook strived so hard to do his job well.

There was a certain artistry in cooking. A pinch of herbs here and sprinkle of spice there spelled the difference between success and failure. Because a submarine's crew's mess was confined and because the men ate from platters of food, the presentation became important. Preparing tasty and appetizing food involved how the food looked. Making food look appetizing takes time and time was always the submarine cook's enemy. Food quality was so often a function of the raw material. Selecting and ordering the right food in the right quantity ranked at least as important as the preparation of the food for serving.

There was a body of knowledge required to be a submarine cook. It was often thought that anyone could follow a recipe and put out a good meal. That impression was far from the truth. For example, coffee is best brewed at 209 degree F. but should be served at 185 degrees. When tea boils it produces steam which turns the tea bitter. Cocoa is just as flavorful using condensed milk as fresh milk. Submariners prefer dry heat cooking using roasts, ribs, beef steak, pot roast or braised pork chops. The time lag between cooked meat cutting and serving should never exceed seven minutes. There is a considerable difference between broilers, capons, fryers and roasters, but to most of us they are all just chickens. The good cook knew the difference and kept in his head a huge amount of detail pertaining to cooking temperatures, ingredient amounts and sequence of actions.

A ship's cook had a vocabulary derived from descriptors in the Standard Navy Recipe Service. Words such as savory, seasoned, chilled, fresh, Julienne, hearty, spiced, piping-hot, juicy, pan-fried, au gratin, colorful, grilled and simmered quickly became a part of the cook's working vocabulary. He learned the difference between Iceberg, Boston, Romaine, Chicory, Escarole and Watercress lettuce and he knew what dressings go best with what types of lettuce.

The SRC survey revealed the chief difficulties of the job. With near unanimity the number one difficulty was cited as exhaustion. The cook kept long hours. He was often under-staffed which placed an even greater pressure on getting the food onto the tables on schedule. The job was always grueling, it was often frustrating and was sometimes dangerous. Rough sees plagued the submarine cook more than most jobs. Hot grease and oil sloshing about can produce severe burns. Of course, snorkeling killed the chances of any successful baked goods. Making it all the worse was the misplaced sense of humor of those in the control room who delighted in hand-cycling the head valve at the baker's critical moments or running with a big up angle to make his cakes wedge-shaped.

Other difficulties involved the planning, organization and storing of food, the preparation and service of food during adverse conditions, the record keeping, and trying to please all the crew members all the time. Specifically, difficulties included baking while snorkeling, working while seasick, holding on while trying to prepare food, serving meals on time, record keeping, making up the menu, trying to maintain quality without fresh food and putting up with blowing sanitaries just as the cooks, who ate last, sat down to eat.

When the seas were rough enough, the menu was set aside for easy fixings and the crew's mess was open on a twenty four hour basis.

Submarine cooks became so accustomed to food preparation in adverse conditions that the problem of heavy seas was overcome by serving meals that could be eaten on the run and that would not slide off a table. When the boat was rolling fifty to sixty degrees and plunging into mountainous waves sandwiches were prepared and left on trays for those hearty souls whose stomachs could stand up to the sea sickness. Sometimes simple meals could be served such as hot dogs, beans, cold cuts, and chili. Soup could be served in cups and men liked to crush crackers into the soup to give it stability. In almost every compartment could be found a box of Saltine crackers.

Of course, all these adversities only applied to the diesel boats. One nuclear sailor responded to SRC's question about heavy seas by saying, "When we began to roll we just went deeper."

If the above description of life as a cook on a diesel fleet type or Guppy boat seems a bit rough, take a look at what being a cook on an S boat involved. One responding S boat submarine cook told the following:

"There was never enough fresh water on the S boats for normal usage. The crew's use of fresh water was limited to drinking-water and food preparation. The only exception to the rule was that the ship's cook was allowed to 'wash up' before going to work in the galley. For this purpose he was rationed seven cups of water in a bucket. The wash-up consisted of washing the face, neck, arms and hands using socks or skivvies as a rag. Next, the same water was used for the trunk, legs and feet. Last came the privates, then the socks and skivvies themselves were washed. It is said that some cooks then added the used water to the coffee urn after the socks and skivvies had been squeezed back into the bucket."

In spite of all the negatives, submarine cooks continued to take great pride in their work and would never have changed their rate for another. The Navy recognized good food preparation by sometimes listing the command's name on the recipe card and by presenting awards to meritorious boats.

CHAPTER 7
FAVORITE BEEF DISHES

The results of the questionnaire illustrated the uncontested collective opinion of submarine cooks that their crews liked beef better than any other form of meat. True, lobsters topped even the beef in popularity, but in the practical sense lobster could not be afforded as a daily diet, nor even if it could, the men would have quickly demanded a return to beef as the main-stay of submarine meals.

Roast beef topped even steaks as the most popular form of beef. Crews liked lots of gravy over their accompanying mashed potatoes and this accounts for the second place showing of steaks on the popularity survey. While in port steaks were normally Porterhouse, T-bone or other boned and fat-striated beef. When the perimeter fat-lined steaks were grilled they gave off delicious smells that made their way into the control room. And when stacked on serving platters they glistened.

When taking on food for a patrol the steaks were normally trimmed of bone and much of their fat. This was intended to save space, but it reduced the extravagance of the meal. Frozen steaks and roasts lost a little of their taste. Worse, if the meat was not stored properly with adequate ventilation in the freeze locker the meat could partially spoil or freeze-burn. During the Second World War cooks learned the tricks of maximizing storage space use and of insuring uniform freezing of meat.

Ground shoulder of beef was used for hamburgers and no matter how gourmet the meals, submariners continued to like the great American sandwich. Meat loaf was another popular meal which combined pork and beef or could be made using just beef. Last but not least, it should be stated that SOS was a beef-in-sauce dish that was the mainstay of submarine breakfasts.

Corned beef and boiled beef were low on the popularity scale, but chipped beef which also came in cans was the meat ingredient for creamed beef, the other half of the breakfast mainstay.

CHARLES MCGUCKIN'S SLIDERS
(Grilled Hamburgers, J-39)

The following recipe is from the 1939 edition of the U.S. Navy Cookbook. Hamburgers were a favorite of Second World War submariners. Here is Chuck McGuckin (MM2)'s recipe for Sliders. He served aboard the Chivo (SS-341), Cobbler (SS-344) and George Washington, (SSBN-598).

The following will yield about five patties:

Ingredients	Measure/Weight	Method
Bread crumbs	1/2 cup	Combine salt, pepper, garlic powder and bread crumbs together and mix well.
Ground beef, lean	1 and 1/2 lb.	Add 1 egg to the mixture, combine until well blended into a paste.
Salt	1/4 tsp	
Pepper	1/2 tsp	
Garlic powder	1/2 tsp	
Egg, whole	1 large	Combine ground beef and bread mixture together and blend well. Do not over mix!
		Measure out approx 3/4 cup of the meat and form into patties.
		Grill on a lightly greased 350 deg F frying pan, or griddle until juices run clear or degree of doneness is reached. (approx 8-10 minutes)

Chuck's advice is as follows:
"To add authenticity, place a bucket of diesel fuel near where you intend to eat. The added aroma will bring back the memories of eating in the after battery and enhance the digestive process. You may also add a couple drops of 2110 T.H. hydraulic oil to your favorite beverage. This will simulate the ever-present hydraulic leak from the main induction above the crew's mess tables. (Nukes: eat your heart out!)

"This (J-39) appeared to be a 1940 era recipe. By the time I joined the Navy, they had gone to frozen patties so I attempted to use as much of the original recipe as I could substituting bread crumbs for bread and using some garlic powder for added taste. You may omit the garlic if you desire and/or use flavored bread crumbs. The 1939 edition of the United States Navy Cook Book called for two 2 and 1/2 ounce patties, which I increased to 1/3 pound. This cooks down to a little more than a 4 ounce burger like a quarter pounder when grilled, which is just about what the original recipe called for. So instead of two small burgers, you get one bigger burger. I used a measuring cup to portion the meat and found 3/4 of a cup is just about right.

Cooking time varied depending on the heat source. It is important to cook hamburger until the juices run clear so the cooking time is only a guide and may be either more of less."

JAMES BAUMAN'S BRAISED BEEF (J-9)
TAKEN FROM 1944 U.S. NAVY COOKBOOK

Submarine cooks during the Second World War kept a good supply of galley tools, but for this recipe they had to send a mess cook back to the engine rooms to borrow a twelve inch Philips screwdriver. That reason alone makes this braised beef recipe special, but the home version was produced by both James and Dottie Bauman. James commanded the submarines Cavalla (AGSS-244) and Sea Owl (SS-405) during the late 1960s.

Ingredients	Measure/Weight	Method
Beef, round roast	4 pounds, tied	Punch holes in beef with big screwdriver. Enlarge with fingers. Push pieces of pork into holes.
Salt pork,	4 pcs, 1/2 in.dia x 3 in.	
Potato, diced	1 small	
Carrot, diced	1 medium	
Turnip, diced	1 small	
Onion, diced	1 medium	
Celery leaves,	2 ounces	
Garlic cloves, minced	2 medium	
Bayleaf	1	
Flour	About 2 cups	Dredge beef and vegetables in flour. Brown beef and veggies in fry pan on range. Add oil if necessary. Stir frequently Transfer to baking pan, add stock and cover with aluminum foil. (or use roaster pan). Place in 350 degree oven. Turn beef and baste every 30 minutes. Check for desired doneness, (normally one hour, forty five minutes - 170 degrees internal temp.)

James suggests the following.
"Place the beef on a board to rest before slicing. Strain the vegetables from the broth and pour off the fat. Arrange meat onto a platter and serve with broth as a gravy. This will serve about six to eight people.

"Making holes in the beef and inserting the pork was difficult. We redid the recipe dicing the salt pork and tossing it with the vegetables. This worked just as well. Also, celery flakes seemed to work just as well. None of our neighbors could tell the difference."

JIMMY GUNTER'S ROAST BEEF (J-4)

A roast beef recipe is a simple one, but a crucial one. Roast beef stands as the historical submarine silver medal winner for popularity. There is no denying the crew's preference for good beef over all other meats. The tastiest beef flavors came from roasts. Jimmy served in submarines during the 1960s and used the Standard Navy Recipes of the era. He qualified on the Quillback (SS-424) and served on Grenadier (SS-525). His version of submarine roast beef uses a few more spices to enhance the beef flavor than the standard Navy recipe. The following will serve according to the size of the roast and the appetite of the eaters.

Ingredients	Measure/Weight	Method
Beef, boneless, roast	3 to 4 pounds	Wash the roast, then place it in a small roasting pan.
Water	1 cup	Pour water over roast slowly.
Salt	1 tsp	
Pepper	1/2 tsp	
Onion, finely chopped or onion powder	1/2 tsp	
Garlic, finely chopped or garlic powder	1/2 tsp	Mix dry ingredients thoroughly. Divide the dry ingredients in half. Sprinkle 1/2 of dry ingredients over dampened roast and press into surface. Cover roast with pan lid or foil Oven cook roast at 300 deg F. to desired doneness (normally about one hour per side). Turn the roast and sprinkle with remaining ingredients. Cook for same amount of time before turning. Test with meat thermometer. Let stand for 30 minutes before carving.

If a larger roast is used, punch a few holes in the roast and insert diced garlic cloves. If the roast is over done it will be difficult to slice properly. A gravy may be made from the drippings by using pre-mixed flour and water. Scrape the pan bottom to get the full flavor. Arrange the slices on a serving tray, pour gravy over slices and place before the hungry crew members in your family.

NICK LOUQUE'S GINGER POT ROAST (J-11)

This recipe for Ginger Pot Roast originally came from the Navy Standard Recipe Service and was developed in the 1950s. It quickly became a favorite of submariners where it added just the right zest to basic beef dishes. Nick Louque qualified on the Robert E. Lee, (SSBN-601) and served this recipe with dehydrated mashed potatoes, rice or grits. It was only reasonable that grits should be served on a submarine bearing the name of the South's greatest general.

Ingredients	Measure/Weight	Method
Beef, boneless, pot roast	3 or 4 pounds	Preheat oven to 275 deg F. Salt and pepper beef. Melt shortening over med-high heat. Add seasoned beef. Brown well on all sides. Add garlic, onions, tomatoes, stock and seasonings to beef.
Salt	1 tsp	
Pepper	1/2 tsp	
Shortening	2 tsp	
Garlic powder	1/2 tsp	
Onions, dehydrated	3 tbsp	
Tomatoes, canned	One 24 oz. can	
Stock, beef or water	4 cups	
Bouillon cubes	3 to 6	
Ginger, ground	1 and 1/2 tsp	
Thyme	1/2 tsp	Stir and bring to boil. Transfer to preheated oven Cook in heavy skillet or Dutch oven for three hours. Remove beef and set aside. Add flour to stock, stirring constantly and bring to a simmer. Place beef in serving dish and smother with stock.
Bay leaves	1 leaf	
Flour	3 tbsp	

The recipe can be prepared using any kind of covered baking dish, however, a heavy skillet or Teflon lined deep baking tub works best.

If the dish is served with mashed potatoes the beef should be beside the potatoes. If it is served with rice or grits it may sit astride the underlying rice or grits.

CHARLES BROWN'S GRAVIED BEEF ON RICE

A recipe for beef that is a distant cousin to Beef Stroganoff is Charlie's favorite dinner. It is not difficult to make and is a real savory delight. It is a two-pot dinner; one for the rice and the other for the meat sauce. The recipe is enough for about eight people.

Ingredients	Measure/Weight	Method
Steak, flank	1 2 pound steak	Cut the flank steak into cubes about inch square. Fry the beef in a skillet using a small amount of oil.
Onion, diced	2 onions, med	
Celery, chopped	4 stalks	
Salt	pinch	Add salt, celery and onion when beef is browned. Continue cooking until onions are clear.
Pepper	pinch	
Sauce, Worcestershire	6 dashes	
Sauce, soy	6 dashes	
Bouquet, kitchen	6 dashes	Add seasoning.
Stock, beef	1 can	
Flour, sifted	2 tbsp	Add flour to stock and mix thoroughly. Pour stock and flour into skillet. Continue to cook until the gravy is correct consistency.
Rice, white	1/2 cup	Boil or steam rice until soft. Ladle beef chunks and sauce over rice.

Stew meat in cubes may be used instead of flank steak. In both cases the meat should be well browned and then well cooked in sauce. Charlie suggests that a green salad with blue cheese dressing be served with the meal.

CHARLES BROWN'S CORNED BEEF AND CABBAGE (J-26)

This is a simple recipe. It was one of the long patrol options. Corned beef had a long shelf life and could be relied upon to offer an appetizing meal when all the fresh foods had been consumed. A submarine's menu didn't advertise that the cabbage in question was dehydrated and then reconstituted on the day of serving. Fortunately, fresh cabbage can now be used so that the retired submariner can avoid the gluey cabbage of the boats.

Ingredients	Measure/Weight	Method
Beef, corned	1 12 ounce can	
Onion	1 medium	Shred the beef into course hunks. Fry the corned beef and onion until the onion is clear.
Tomato sauce	1 8 ounce can	Add the sauce. Simmer contents.
Cabbage	1 head	Cut cabbage into quarters. Add cabbage to contents. Continue to simmer.
Salt	Pinch	
Pepper	Pinch	Add seasoning.
Rice	1/2 cup	Boil rice separately. Serve the beef and cabbage over a bed of rice.

This quick and easy meal is a favorite of New Englanders during the fall, when the leaves are red and the air is crisp.

FAIRMAN BOCKHORST'S CHICKEN FRIED STEAK

Chicken fried steak hasn't anything to do with chicken. It is a beef dish and was a real favorite for a noon meal. Fairman Bockhorst was an electronics technician who went to nuclear power school in New London from the surface fleet and then went to the USS Pollack (SSN-603). During his eight years on active duty he loved submarine food and this is his recipe for chicken fried steak.

Ingredients	Measure/Weight	Method
Beef, boneless top loin	2 lbs.	Pound the steak with a knife or meat tenderizing hammer.
Egg, beaten	one large	Pour onto plate.
Milk	1 tbsp	
Crackers, saltine crushed	1 cup	
Salt	1 pinch	
Pepper	1 pinch	Mix the dry ingredients in a bowl and pour onto a plate. Dip the beaten meat into the egg and then coat both sides of the meat with the dry ingredients. Brown meat on both sides in hot oil, then turn heat down to simmer, cover the skillet and cook until tender (about 40 to 45 minutes).

Gravy for the meat may be made by removing the meat and adding 1 tablespoon of cool water to 1/4 cup flour. Blend the flour to reduce lumps. Add the water and flour mixture to the drippings. Bring to a boil and simmer until the mixture is the desired consistency.

This recipe should enough for about four.

CHAPTER 8
THE STANDARD NAVY RECIPE SERVICE

It wasn't too long before the Second World War that scientists became aware of the body's need for vitamins and minerals. Nutrition came to center-stage in the armed forces when the need for special rations became apparent. In an effort to insure that naval personnel remained healthy the Navy made nutrition the foundation of its training for the rate of cook.

Where as, in the past, the training of Navy cooks had been perfunctory and on-the-job training was the avenue for advancement it reinforced its schools and required a substantial knowledge before the cook actually started work. In addition, the Navy improved its 1920 cook book. This larger and more complete cook book became the submarine cook's bible. The 1938 version contained recipes and instructions for preparing well-balanced, nutritional meals that were attractive and tasty.

"The Cook Book of the United States Navy", printed in 1938 and revised many times thereafter started with a complete description of proteins, vitamins and minerals. The emphasis of thought was that a Navy fighting man needed energy-producing food to do his job. The first part of the book was also devoted to planning the menu. Not only must the food have been nutritional it must also have been attractive to be eaten in sufficient quantity for the Navy's energy requirements.

Since mathematics was a basic requisite of cooking, tables of weights and measures were presented so the cooks of various size craft could adjust the Navy Cook Book portions to fit the size of the respective crew. The recipes were created for the serving of one hundred men. This fit nicely into the Fleet Type Submarine of the Second World War since the crew of that type of boat ranged between seventy five and one hundred.

At the beginning of the Second World War food preservation had seen many recent innovations. Quick freezing had been invented and a few frozen foods were available. Some foods were dehydrated and could be reconstituted by adding water. For long range submarines these innovations meant that men could be fed nutritious meals for longer periods at sea.

Once again it should be emphasized that submarines of this era as well as those of today were and are limited not by fuel, but by the amount of food they can carry.

An example of dried food used during the Second World War (and of the present) is powdered eggs. Here is the recipe for scrambled eggs as described on page 63 of the 1944 edition.

```
Eggs, whole, powdered. . . . . 6 pounds
Water. . . . . . . . . . . . . . . . . . . . 2 gallons
Salt. . . . . . . . . . . . . . . . . . . . . 6 tablespoons
Pepper. . . . . . . . . . . . . . . . . . .1 tablespoon
```

Fat, melted. . . . . 1 and 1/2 quarts

Instructions called for melting the fat and whipping the water and eggs into a froth.

If this sounds unappetizing, it was. The men grumbled about the food and on long duration patrols endured it since nothing else was available.

To continue the example into current submarine food service, eggs are no longer stored in their shells. Their contents are in containers that make better use of space and the quantity is such that most FBM assignments can be carried with egg preparation not unlike that in your home. Powdered eggs are still carried in limited quantity for emergencies, but food preservation techniques have improved dramatically over the past thirty years.

The rest of "The Cook Book of the United States Navy" was devoted to recipes and preparation instructions. This book remained as the sole resource for submarine cooks until the late forties when the first Standard Navy Recipe cards appeared. These were intended to take the place of the cook book. They were colored according to type of item and came in a small wooden box which quickly became soaked in the fats of the galley. During the fifties the boxes were replaced with metal ones and the cards were periodically updated to keep current with improved recipes and a greater variety of manufactured foods. The Navy issued submarine supplements to the recipes and gave credit to the boats that submitted them to BuSandA.

In the early nineties the Navy went entirely to computers. The Navy Recipe Service currently is programmed and menus are made from selections that are surprisingly similar to those on the earlier recipe cards.

The recipes in this publication are tuned to both the original cook books and Standard Navy Recipes from the nineteen sixties. The letter and number designators following the name of the recipe denotes the recipe number in the Standard Navy Recipe Service. Where none appear the recipe is a product of a submarine cook's innovation.

The question arises as to how closely the submarine cooks stuck to the recipes. A concomitant question is how often the cooks substituted their own recipes from personal sources for those of the Recipe Service. SRC's study of forty two submarine cooks described in the introduction tells us that:

> Submarine cooks followed the Standard Navy Recipes with very little deviation seventy one percent of the time.
>
> Submarine bakers followed the Standard Navy Recipes for baked goods ninety three percent of the time.
>
> Submarine cooks cooked from memory of personal recipes only about nineteen percent of the time.

Not every cook was enthusiastic about the Navy's Recipe Service. A few relied exclusively on their memory. Warren Rucker, a cook on the Grampus during the 1950s remembers the following:

"The older cooks thought the cards were a joke, but I (twenty years old) was required to use them from time to time. One meal I prepared using the cards brought a threat from our executive officer that he'd throw me overboard along with the next meal I prepared using the cards."

When one reads about foraging it is usually within the context of soldiers living off the land. Sherman's march through Georgia to the sea was an example of how an entire army could deliberately cut itself off from logistical supplies and sustain itself nutritionally by taking what it needed from luckless farmers.

What isn't well known is that American submariners, being innovative fishermen, did their fair share of foraging for food. Jim Tierney tells us, "While at Key West we would trap off the beach or off the pier for longuista. We would half fill a 35 gallon trash can with longuista, take the load back to the pier, and hit the trash can with live steam from the pier. When cooked, we twisted the tails from the bodies and brought them down to the crew's mess where the duty section spent an hour dipping fresh meat into melted butter. I never had a tastier meal."

The early missile boats that had the miserable job of spending months in the far reaches of the northern Pacific augmented their meals with fresh king crab legs. The boys in the engine rooms made wire traps which were baited and laid onto the bottom sea bed while the boat crept on the surface at one third. The next night the boat would return, spot the tiny buoys and haul up many large crabs. Once again the drawn butter and crab meat made for a great feast.

It should be noted that underway submarines were very poor platforms for regular line fishing. No one wanted to break rig for dive to throw over a doubtful baited hook. Crabs and lobsters seemed to be the only real submarine foraging bounty.

The advent of the nuclear submarine which remains submerged pretty much did away with foraging.

The cards (Navy Recipe Service) were best used as a starting point. They provided the submarine cook with the foundation for a dish and the competent cook added or deleted ingredients as he saw fit. This is where the art of cooking made itself known.

The basic question pertaining to the preparation of real cuisine attends to a cooking talent as being an art or a science. This is a never-ending debate, however, in so far as submarine cooks are concerned nearly all of them started with no particular talent and often with little interest. Their skill arose from the desire to do a job well. The Standard Navy Recipes gave the cook the foundation to prepare wholesome and nutritious meals with great consistency. A few, some of whom became legendary in their own time, branched out into creative endeavors that turned ordinary submarines into culinary laboratories. Creativity was encouraged when successful, but when things went wrong the cook quickly retreated back the Standard Navy Recipes. A few who had a hidden talent became famous for their particular dishes. Those who were successful became the darlings of the crew and captain and enjoyed a very special place within the ship's social structure.

CHAPTER 9
THREE PORK AND HAM DISHES

Cured ham was a popular alternative to beef and was always well received by submariners. It could be served as the meat entree of the noon or evening meals or could be served as the meat accompaniment to eggs to order. Since it could be stored for lengthy periods in the cool locker it was often taken aboard while preparing for a patrol. In addition, canned ham was abundant and could be stored in relatively cool places such as bilges or between torpedo tubes.

Left over ham was made into soups and salads. It could also be used with macaroni and cheese as an alternate entree.

Ham could be prepared in a variety of ways depending on the glaze. The most popular was the "honey" glaze made from brown sugar and spices.

When Hormel started pressing diced shoulder hunks into small cans and calling it Spam the whole military world changed. Since it was portable, easy to open, tasty and nutritious the American military bought it in huge quantity. Its over-use gave it a bad name and submariners were included with those who criticized the meat product, but they willingly ate it with their eggs to order. Spam was a good meat product to use with noodles or macaroni in salads and side dishes.

Pork was served in various forms, but for the most part, submariners ate pork chops as the entree. These were often thick enough to be sliced, butterflied and stuffed with a dressing. This extended the meat and offered an alternative to the plain pork chop. As with the case for beef steaks pork chops and lamb chops were deboned before storing in the freezer for a patrol.

Pork roasts rated high with submariners and accompanying gravies were much appreciated.

AL CADDY'S BAKED HAM, VIRGINIA STYLE (J-77)

Al Caddy had been in the Navy for seven years before he volunteered for submarines and went to submarine school. He served on the Sennet (SS- 408) and qualified on the Clamagore (SS-343). He then went to the Tench (SS-417) and later to the Rock (SSG-274) in San Diego. He remembered the ham served aboard his boats and constructed the following recipe to replicate what he recollected about the taste of the sweet and tender meat. The recipe below will feed about four people.

Ingredients	Measure/Weight	Method
Ham, smoked, boned and tied.	1 and 1/2 pounds	Place ham fat-side up in roasting pan.
Sugar, brown packed	3/4 cup	Bake at about 300 deg F for 2 hours. Remove ham from oven, remove skin and string.
Vinegar	3.2 ounces	
Mustard, dry	1/2 ounce	
Pepper, cayenne	1/4 tsp	
Bread crumbs, fine	3.2 ounces	Score fat in 1 inch squares. Make a paste of brown sugar, vinegar, mustard, pepper and bread crumbs. Rub the paste into the ham.
Cloves, whole	6 to 8 cloves	Stick one clove in each square of scored fat. Return ham to oven and bake at 325 deg F until the internal temperature reaches 170 Deg F, (approximately one hour).
		Allow ham to set for 30 minutes before carving.

Precooked, boneless, casing-type ham may be substituted for the smoked ham. If so, bake until internal temperature is 145 Deg F is reached. For a varied taste, try your baked ham with peanut butter glaze. Combine the following to make a smooth paste: 1/2 cup peanut butter, pinch of cinnamon, pinch of cloves, 1 tsp sugar, 1 tbsp cornstarch, 1 ounce of butter, a pinch of salt, 2 tbsp brown sugar and 3 oz. of water. Pour the paste over the ham as described above and bake at 325 Deg F.

NICK DIRKX'S BARBECUED POT ROAST OF PORK (J-88)

This simple recipe is the best application of Nick's barbecue sauce (Chapter 3). It is a beautiful entrée that is simple to prepare and savory with noodles or potatoes.

Ingredients	Measure/Weight	Method
Pork, Fresh, shoulder	2 pounds	Trim excess fat from roast. Rub roast with vegetable oil. Place in a heavy skillet. Brown the roast on both sides over high heat.
Sauce, barbecue	1/4 cup	Brush sauce onto pork roast. Coat the roast well. Cover and simmer to doneness of about 180 deg F. The roast should be very tender. Slice into thin diagonally cut pieces. Arrange slices on serving platter and baste with excess sauce.

Roast pork is a dish that is lean and requires a sauce. For a Hawaiian flavor add a small amount of pineapple juice to the sauce.

CHARLES BROWN'S KIDNEY BEAN MACARONI WITH HAM
(J-76)

This publication would not be complete were it to not include at least one of the recipes used by submarine cooks to provide a healthy meal during the latter days of a patrol. Such a meal had to built around what was available. Dry goods such as macaroni and beans could be combined with what was left in the freezer or cool box. Often the beef would be eaten in preference to the ham. To stretch the remaining meat, ham was often combined with helpers such as macaroni and beans. Here is Charles Brown's version of a long patrol meal reduced to family size.

Ingredients	Measure/Weight	Method
Ham, butt or shank	1	
Kidney beans	1 pound	Day before preparation screen beans for foreign matter. Wash them thoroughly and soak overnight. Boil the ham until done, about one hour. Place the ham stock in the refrigerator overnight.
Macaroni, elbow	1 pound	Remove the fat from the ham and discard. Dice the ham into small pieces. Remove the fat from the stock and discard. Drain the kidney beans and place in a large pot. Add the ham stock and ham bones.
Onions, chopped	2	
Tomatoes, canned	2 medium cans	
Celery, chopped	6 stalks	
Salt	pinch	
Pepper	pinch	
Sauce, Worcestershire	3 dashes	Add onion, celery, canned tomatoes and spices.
Water	enough to cover beans.	Add water to pot so that contents are covered. Simmer until beans and macaroni are soft. Add seasoning to taste.

The ham and beans will automatically cook correctly if the boiling mixture is tuned to the macaroni. Don't let the macaroni over-cook. Test it every five minutes. Each elbow should be soft but not mushy.

CHAPTER 10
FOOD STORAGE ABOARD SUBMARINES

Submarines were always cramped. Even modern submarines have difficulty in storing the food necessary for a long patrol. Fleet ballistic missile submarines are long and wide with special accommodations for frozen foods, and chilled foods. They have lockers of adequate size designed so that food access is tuned to computerized menu planning. With escape trunks removed there are two points of entrance to the nuclear powered boats both of which accommodate large palates of food that are power-winched into the internal spaces.

Nuclear fast attack submarines are not so well suited to long patrols. They still largely depend on hand labor to get the food into the submarine where it is stored in every vacant space not unlike that of the diesel boats. As each succeeding generation of submarines is designed, improvements are made in food storage, but the fact remains that food is the number one limiting factor in patrol duration. An interesting paradox is the inverse relation to space design and the limitation of food storage availability. As designers get better use out of every inch of space in a submarine, so the flexibility of stashing cans of food in unlikely places diminishes.

Bilges and decks were the number one informal storage spaces in diesel boats. Canned goods could be shoved under lockers, outboard of the engines, between torpedo tubes, in showers and heads and even in the overhead. Cocoa packages went into personal lockers. Forward and after battery berthing decks were covered with number ten canned goods crates. Hogan's Alley (After battery crew's berthing port longitudinal bunk access) sometimes had two layers of canned goods. Crew members squeezed into lower bunks with canned goods stacked above them.

There was some science to this hap-hazard approach to food storage. For example, coffee and flower tended to be placed in the torpedo room bilges and outboard of the engines. Neither heat nor dampness permeated the metal containers to the detriment of the contents, (provided the boat lacked a snorkel). Sugar was stowed in dry water-ways. It was often stored forward of the main motors. Cans of evaporated milk just fit under the bunks in crew's berthing. Potatoes in sacks were best stowed between machinery in the pump room or in torpedo skids, and of course, in the crew's mess benches. The escape trunk made a fine storage place, but access to its contents could only be through the upper hatch which required breaking rig for dive. Fresh eggs were stored in torpedo room bilges. They were stacked 30 to a 20 egg carton. Radiomen hunched over their keys as they sat on number ten canned goods.

All of this discomfort had only to be endured during the first month or so of a patrol. The cooks planned the menu so that Guppy sailors could eat their way through the more objectionable space-taking foods as early in the patrol as possible. At the end of a patrol there was lots of room, but the menu was reduced to macaroni and cheese.

Nuclear fast attack boats are not afforded the flexibility of such informal storage practices, since many of the spaces are either not there to begin with or have been taken by electronic equipment. Having said that, deck space, personal lockers, showers and heads are still full of dry rations at the start of a patrol.

One diesel boat cook lamented that getting ready for a patrol was, "a real project." This understatement commented on the cumbersome supply system and reliance on ship's crew to get the food into every nook and cranny of the submarine.

When Guppies were designed they doubled their battery capacity. Some of the additional space for the added battery cells came from the cool and frozen food lockers. Even so, the cooks tried to keep ninety days of provisions on hand. The freeze box was about six feet by six feet with a seven foot overhead. Cooks learned to debone meat before cold-storing it. The Hawkbill (SSN-666) had an eight foot by twelve foot frozen food locker. This was an improvement, but was still not adequate for long patrols.

To increase the frozen capacity many boats converted their cool boxes to freeze boxes. When they were retained as cool boxes cooks removed eggs from containers to save space. A cool box could carry enough food (with dry goods stored elsewhere) for sixty to ninety days at sea. Submarines on northern runs often used their escape trunks as a second cool box. Eggs were sometimes stored in nets and slung in the trunks in such a way as to allow access from the lower hatch.

The following is an anecdote from a submariner of the Second World War, Captain R. C. Latham. It was printed in a volume titled "Dolphin Tales" edited by Mariette W. Irwin and Julie A. Joa in 1971.

"This is a story about the submarine which augmented its supply of fresh food by stowing potatoes in a deck locker which was reached by a hatch in the after end of the bridge superstructure, (cigarette deck). Although the locker flooded when the boat dove, the submarine didn't dive very often or very deep on their way to patrol and it didn't hurt the spuds. By the time they reached enemy waters, the locker was empty. The procedure worked fine. This submarine had a skipper who was known throughout the service for his ability to verbally chastise a miscreant in flaming prose. It was the skipper's habit to pace back and forth in the confined area at the after end of the bridge deck. One day the mess cook asked for permission to come to the bridge and it was granted. He came up with an empty tureen, went back to the after end of the bridge, lifted the hatch and by lying on his stomach and stretching , was just able to reach the spuds in the bottom of the locker. He filled the tureen and took it below, leaving the hatch open because he had to return to fill the tureen once more. While he was gone the skipper came on deck and commenced his pacing back and forth and, of course, fell into the spud locker.

'Who the blankety blank left this blankety blank spud locker hatch open?' he bellowed upon climbing out. About then the mess cook returned and immediately became the recipient of one of the classical verbal barrages. It was a humdinger and the watch on the bridge listened in awe, further inspiring the skipper. Finally the old man finished and added, 'Don't ever leave that blankety blank hatch open again.' With great dignity he turned and once again stepped into the open hatch."

It should be noted that fleet type boats had free flooding superstructures. These afforded space for anything that could withstand sea pressure and salt water erosion. Nuclear submarines have either very little or no superstructure (and commensurately, no hatches into which a captain might fall).

The capability to serve nutritional meals during the waning days of a long patrol largely depended on the meticulous attention to detail in the storing of food prior to the patrol. The computer is an invaluable tool in this regard, but before the use of computers on submarines careful inventories of foods and their locations throughout the submarine spelled the difference between endless macaroni and balanced meals in the tenth week of a patrol.

Smart cooks hoarded certain fresh foods with long shelf lives. For example, they mixed a few fresh potatoes with dehydrated ones and got a fresh taste that amazed crew members. Desserts were made using powdered ice cream mixed with canned cherries. The result was a fresh tasting dessert. During the last days of a patrol the cook might break out of the freeze locker frozen strawberries, steaks, and whole frozen corn for meals between the more drab items of canned goods.

Fresh foods were consumed at a predictable rate:
    Fresh fruits lasted only about a week.
    Fresh vegetables lasted about two weeks.
    Milk lasted about three weeks.
    Butter lasted about four weeks.

After about a month all fresh items had been consumed. Eggs lasted about fifty five to sixty days. Canned fruits and vegetables replaced the fresh ones as the patrol progressed. Powdered and dehydrated foods replaced the canned goods as those ran out. Pickles and olives helped the illusion that freshness was still possible. One cook suggested that adding a little vanilla to the powdered milk mix gave it a pleasant flavor. It was essential to mix the milk and chill it about twelve hours before use. This also seemed to be true for powdered eggs. When mixed the day before the eggs were much more palatable. Powdered milk and eggs when used in baking were a challenge for the best of bakers. Dehydrated onions and peppers gave otherwise drab soups a real sparkle. Hot chocolate mix in powder form could be made into syrups and toppings.

Food consumption was carefully planned by the cooks. When a boat was late in being relieved on station the menu planning got very dicey. Mess cooks were known to scavenge through the boat's hidden crevices in search of some over-looked morsel. During the last days at sea menu planning was a function of what was left. The cook's job was to be creative in combining the few remaining foods into something flavorful.

If the above sounds like it may have involved some serious hardships take a look at the S-boats. One of SRC's respondent cooks wrote the following:

"There was never enough fresh water on the S-boats for normal usage. The crew's use of fresh water was limited to drinking water and food preparation. The only exception to the rule was that the ship's cook was allowed to 'wash up' before going to work in the galley. For this purpose he was rationed seven cups of water in a bucket. The wash-up consisted of rag-washing the face, neck, arms and hands. Next, the same water was used for the trunk, legs and feet. Last came the privates, then the socks and skivvies. It is said that some cooks then added the used water to the coffee urn."

The Sirago (SS-485) went on extended special operations and the lead cook neglected to take aboard enough salt. Being an imaginative sailor he simply took a few boxes of salt tablets from the engine rooms, ground up the salt tablets and put the powder into the salt shakers. Of course the tablets had been colored purple by the Navy and so the salt in the shakers was also purple. One the young crew members who must have had a pre-condition of mild paranoia took into his mind that the lead cook and the commissary officer were trying to poison the crew. He reported this to the chief of the boat who in turn reported the news to the executive officer. There were a few anxious moments for the cook and commissary officer, but the rumor was quickly put to rest and the young man was transferred off the boat when it returned to Norfolk. The point taken by the lead cook was that no matter how hard he tried to get everything on board there would always be something missing that would get him in trouble.

CHAPTER 11
CHICKEN, A NEVER-ENDING FAVORITE

Poultry in submarines was restricted to chicken and turkey. Whole birds were normally served in port because they were not space efficient. When submarines took them aboard they were normally frozen and this took a great deal of freezer space. They could not be deboned and therefore the amount of meat actually available from poultry was not efficient in terms of nutrients per measured weight.

As frozen turkey and chicken in rolls or filets became available they could be economically stored and served while on patrol, but the cost was comparatively high. Canned turkey and chicken was also available and this was often a preferable option in terms of storage.

Roast turkey was served in the form of a rolled, boneless roast. Chicken was most often served as a meat mixture. This included creamed chicken, Chicken ala King, Chicken in Casserole or Chicken Stew.

Whole chicken and turkey was served when in port, but the amount of work required in preparation was large. Since the oven in a fleet type or Guppy submarine was not large, only two or three turkeys or about eight chickens could be roasted at one time. This meant that oven-fresh meals to an entire crew required continuous use of the oven for long periods. Christmas and Thanksgiving meals required turkey and it was too American to ignore even though it was difficult. Dressings were made and menus for these occasions show cranberry sauce, sweet potato pie and pumpkin pie as being the traditional favorites.

When oven baked chicken was prepared it could be spiced in a variety of ways including curry, pineapple and sugar. Chicken was often pan fried and this too was done with a variety of spices. Southern fried Chicken was a top favorite with the crew.

LIN MARVIL'S CREAMED CHICKEN (L-13)

Lin qualified on the Redfish (SS-395) and served on the Charr (SS-328). He tried to remember the exact dish from his days on the Charr, but he only remembers eating lots of chicken. He was in submarines from 1962 through 1968. He gives most of the credit for the conversion and recipe additions to his wife, Omega.

Ingredients	Measure/Weight	Method
Chicken, whole or breasts	Approx. 2 lb.	A whole boned chicken should yield about two cups of diced meat after cooking.
		Cook chicken until tender. Cut into 1 inch cubes.
Butter, melted	2 tbsp	
Flour	2 tbsp	
Salt	pinch	
Pepper	pinch	Melt butter. Blend in seasoned flour to make roux. Do not brown.
Chicken stock	1 cup	
Milk	1/2 cup	Heat the stock and milk. Gradually add to roux.
Cumin	1/2 tsp	
Celery, finely chopped	1 stalk	Add cumin and celery to mix. Cook about 10 minutes until thickened. Stir frequently.

Serve creamed chicken over toast, rice or pasta. Sprinkle with paprika to garnish. Add a sprig of parsley for color.

HOWARD DACHS' ROAST CHICKEN (L-5,L-22)

Howard Dachs qualified on the USS Sea Robin (SS-407).

Roast chicken with bread dressing was a sort of delicacy on submarines. For the cook it represented a challenge in that the birds had to prepared, cooked and carved. While carving a chicken is no big deal for a family it was a considerable task for the cook serving about one hundred men. It took fifteen to twenty chickens to feed a crew while at sea. A steward was handed four cooked chickens and it was he who carved for the officers. Since the captain was served first he took his favorite pieces and the junior officer or officer coming off watch ate the parts of the chicken not eaten by his comrades.

Ingredients	Measure/Weight	Method
Chicken, fryer	1	Wash and clean chicken, cut it into quarters.
Salt	1/2 tsp	
Pepper	1/2 tsp	
Paprika	1/2 tsp	Sprinkle chicken with dry ingredients.
Shortening, liquid	1/4 cup	Rub chicken with shortening.
		Place chicken skin side up in roasting pan. Roast uncovered at 325 deg F until chicken is tender. Approximately one hour. Baste with drippings. Save drippings for gravy.

A good chicken gravy was made by thoroughly mixing flour with milk, then adding the mixture in small portions to the drippings in the pan while vigorously scraping the pan bottom to release the flavor. If the drippings are really stuck to bottom, pour in a little boiling water. When creamy the gravy was poured into gravy boats and was poured over the accompanying bread dressing at the discretion of the eater.

BREAD DRESSING TO ACCOMPANY ROAST CHICKEN

Howard Dachs' accompanying bread dressing was made as follows:

Ingredients	Measure/Weight	Method
Bread, white	1 loaf	Cut bread into one inch cubes.
Chicken stock	1 can, large	Pour chicken stock over bread.
Onion, chopped	1 medium	
Celery, chopped	2 large stalks	Sauté onions and celery until clear.
Butter	1/4 cup	
Thyme	1 tsp	
Poultry seasoning	2 tsp	
Salt	pinch	
Pepper	pinch	
Water	As needed.	Add seasoning and chopped vegetables to moistened bread mixture. Toss vigorously. Place in greased casserole dish and bake at 350 degF for 30 minutes.

One vegetable normally was served with the roast chicken and dressing. It made a tasty and luxurious meal at reasonable cost.

Variations of the bread dressing recipe include Apple Dressing which was made by sautéing a finely chopped apple with the onion and celery, or by adding a can of creamed corn, or by adding raisins, or by adding bits of sausage.

BILL BENZICK'S
FRIED CHICKEN, MARYLAND STYLE (L-2)

This recipe was developed in the 1950s and was a part of the U.S. Navy's Recipe Service in 1963. Chicken has become a very popular meal during the succeeding decades and this recipe is a great deal better than can be found in restaurants. Bill qualified on the Lizardfish (SS-373) in 1960 and served on the Tunny (SSG-282) during its operations in the northern Pacific.

Ingredients	Measure/Weight	Method
Chickens, fryers,	2	Cut whole chickens into appropriately sized pieces.
White flour	1 and 1/2 cups	Combine dry ingredients and mix well.
Salt	1 tbsp.	
White pepper	1 tsp.	
Paprika	1 tsp.	
Poultry season	1 tsp.	Dredge the chicken pieces in the dry mixture using a large bowl.
Eggs, medium	4	Crack and put in bowl.
Milk,	1 pint	Stir and whip milk and eggs. Dip chicken pieces into this mixture.
Bread crumbs	1/2 pound	Roll moistened chicken pieces in bread crumbs to cover completely. Place pieces in flat baking pan.
Butter	1/4 cup	
Water	2 cups	Add to baking pan before baking. Bake chicken at 375 deg. for approximately 45 minutes or until done. Serve hot on pre-heated plate with garnish.

Drippings left after baking make a good gravy over potatoes or noodles. This recipe will yield about 8 servings.

Bill offers another short recipe for those of you not concerned with cholesterol or fats. While on patrol Tunny shipmates watched movies with special pop-corn. The cook pre-heated the fryer to 400 degrees, and poured in 2 cups of raw pop-corn kernels. When the popped corn rose to the surface he skimmed off the pop-corn with a screen, threw it into a bowl, salted it and put it out to the mess tables. The men loved it, but he comments, "This was a very oily product and probably would not be welcomed in today's culture."

JULIAN POWELL'S BARBECUED CHICKEN
SOUTHERN STYLE (L-6)

Chief Commissaryman Powell was on both diesel and nuclear submarines. He qualified on Chivo (SS-341), and served on Sea Lion (SS-315), and Cavala (SS-244), then went to Tullibee (SSN597) and Sam Houston (SSBN-609). His long service in the submarines makes him one of our authorities on submarine cooking. Here is his special chicken geared down for your family.

Ingredients	Measure/Weight	Method
Butter	1/4 pound	Melt butter in pan and add dry red pepper to butter. Simmer for ten minutes, add remaining ingredients and remove from heat.
Pepper, red, dry	1 tbsp	
Vinegar	1/3 cup	
Sauce, Worcestershire	1 tsp	
Salt	1/4 tsp	
Pepper	1/4 tsp	
Chicken, fryer	1	Wash and clean chicken. Cut into quarters. Place chicken in baking pan, skin side up.
Water	1/4 cup	Add 1/4 cup water to pan. Cover and bake for 30 minutes at 350 deg F. Remove cover, drain liquid and discard. Brush mixed ingredients over chicken parts. Bake another 30 minutes, basting every 10 minutes.

This recipe yields about four portions. Notice that the recipe calls for whole chickens with skin. If the recipe is made without skin the effect of the secret ingredients will be seriously diminished. This is a good recipe for an outdoor grill. The secret is in the frequent bastings, which is a one handed task. The other hand is free to hold a can of beer.

REV. AARON PETER'S CHICKEN POT PIE (L-16)

The Rev. Peters is a USSVi life member as well as a Clamagore Veterans Assn. member. He first served on the Pompon (SS-267) where he qualified in submarines and remembers that chicken pot pie was a favorite of the crew in the fifties. He also served on the Torsk (SS-423), Cutlass (SS-478) and the Theodore Roosevelt (SSBN-600) as well as being a plank owner of the John Marshall (SSBN-611). He is now a Benedictine monk of St. Benedict's Abbey, Atchison, Kansas. Rev. Peters prepared and served his chicken pot pie to thirty five sisters. It is unusual for one of these recipes to have been taste-tested by such a large group, but SRC is appreciative of Rev. Peters' efforts and of the comments from the sisters which appear below. The following recipe is sufficient for about four servings.

Ingredients	Measure/Weight	Method
Chicken, fryer, ready to cook	One whole	Pre-heat oven to 275 deg F.
Water	1 quart	Place chicken or parts into water, boil until flesh falls from bones. Remove chicken and dice the flesh. Skim fat from surface of stock.
Celery, chopped	1/3 cup	
Onions, chopped	1/3 cup	
Carrots, chopped	1/3 cup	
Potatoes, diced	1 potato, med.	Add celery, onions, carrots and potatoes to stock. Continue simmering until vegetables are tender. Drain off chicken stock and set aside.
Peas, frozen	1 package	Place layers of chicken hunks, cooked vegetables and room temperature, uncooked peas into individual soup-sized bowls.
Flour, wheat	1/3 cup	
Salt	1/2 tsp	
Pepper	1/2 tsp	Combine flour and seasoning to stock to make a sauce. Pour sauce over vegetables and chicken. Top with biscuit or pastry of choice and bake as mix directions indicate.

Baking mix is typically made with milk. An easier shell is made with Pillsbury or Bisquick refrigerated dough. The sisters thought the meal served by Rev. Peters was outstanding. They thought it had a "down-home cooking, scrumptious, comfort food taste".

RICHARD GELB'S BRUNSWICK STEW (L-12)

Richard Gelb qualified on and served as ship's cook on the Entemedor (SS-340) during the 1950s. He later served on Croaker (SS-246). He prepared the Brunswick Stew recipe with and without the addition of tomato. According to him, the best recipe is one which uses chicken stock and omits the tomatoes. In this way the chicken flavor is enhanced and balances the taste of the other meat ingredients. The Navy's Brunswick Stew recipe is the only one that combines red and white meats. The recipe is an old Southern tradition.

Ingredients	Measure/Weight	Method
Olive oil	1 tbsp	Canola oil may be used.
Onions	2 medium size	Simmer onions until they are clear.
Beef, cubed	10 ounces	
Veal, cubed	6 ounces	Brown beef and veal in heavy skillet.
Flour	4 tbsp	
Bacon bits	2 tbsp	Add flour and bacon bits. Stir into beef juices, scraping bottom of skillet. Continue to braise the meat.
Vegetable flakes	1 tbsp	
Salt	1 tsp	
Celery, chopped	1 stalk	
Corn, canned	1 15 ounce can	Drain liquid
Worcestershire sauce	1 tbsp	
Pepper	1/4 tsp	Add ingredients to skillet.
Chicken, cubed	1 and 1/4 cup	
Potatoes, diced	1 and 1/4 cup	
Chicken stock	2 and 1/2 cups	Combine ingredients and add to skillet. Add flour one tablespoon at a time to bring viscosity to level of stew. Simmer for 2 to 3 and 1/2 hours. Add seasoning to taste.

This stew is heavy enough to be served with toast and light salad. One may wish to incorporate a white wine to replace one third of the chicken broth.

CHAPTER 12
THE EVOLUTION OF COMMISSARY RECORD-KEEPING

Before 1842 the Navy bought its food from private suppliers and paid for the food with government promissory notes. In that year the Navy established the Bureau of Provisions and Clothing. The Bureau took on the responsibility for Navy personnel pay and the procurement, warehousing and distribution of food and clothing.

At that time the Navy was a fledgling organization and the Bureau competed for recognition as ships continued to buy supplies from the open market. Over the years of that century surprisingly little progress was made in the organization of supply. Under Teddy Roosevelt's administration the Bureau became the Navy's exclusive purchasing agent. This gave it the organizational muscle it needed to be able to coordinate the purchase, acquisition, warehousing, distribution and accounting for all ships and stations of the Navy.

The First World War brought further organizational innovations and the Bureau was renamed the Bureau of Supplies and Accounts or BuSandA. While this organization remains the central supply function of the Navy its methods of food purchase, warehousing, distribution and accounting has dramatically changed.

An appreciation of the sweeping changes that have taken place over the past fifty years can be gained by examining the record keeping practices of the 1950s with those of today. This examination is limited to the activities of submarines and the work of submarine cooks.

One of BuSandA's early achievements was the production of the Navy's first cook book. It was bound in linen covers and about four inches by five inches. It contained suggestions and recipes for cooking on board a ship. Two such recipes from the 1920 edition (Roast Beef and Braised Beef) can be seen in the reproduced actual page of the 1920 edition of the Navy Cook Book located at the end of this chapter.

The Navy Cook Book was expanded both in size and material to the 1938 edition which became the bible for submarine cooks during the Second World War. That book was used in subsequent editions until the development of the Navy's Standard Navy Recipe Service. This service was a set of cards and served as the basic guide for nutrition and menu preparation during the fifties, sixties and seventies. BuSandA even provided a special submarine section of recipes.

By the early nineties the personal computer had become so much a part of the Navy's culture that it began to offer programs having recipes as complimentary material to the printed Standard Navy Recipes. The Navy abandoned the printed Navy recipes and now provides a variety of food procurement and preparation information on computer program. Record keeping is also accomplished on the computer.

With the above historical information as a foundation a view of the records kept by submarine cooks during the 1950s will illustrate the burden placed on cooks in terms of arithmetical calculations and detailed entries. As hard as the submarine cook worked in the galley he was most often to be seen in the crew's mess bent over his records. A good example of the tedious detail involved in record keeping was the reverse side of the menu (Bill of Fare, BuSandA form 333). The weekly menu or bill-of-fare, as the Navy called it, took a lot of time to prepare. But the reverse side was a real nightmare. It was the "Statement of Issues to the General Mess and Cost of Ration Daily". Here the cook spent his time recording the quantity of foods listed on the menu, the unit price of the items in terms of the cost of such foods (to be found in notices from BuSandA) and a recapitulation of the ship's amount spent on food. This was a function of the number of daily rations times the ration allowance per day. The redundant record was subjected to a chorus of complaints from cooks, commissary officers and captains. It was deleted as a requirement for submarines. In addition, the cook prepared a "Daily Ration Memorandum" and a "Daily Ration Memorandum Summary". These forms were sent to the Bureau in an unending flow of paperwork.

The minimum daily serving of food to one man on a submarine was called a ration. This was a carefully defined amount of food split into the seven basic food groups and their subgroups which were intended to insure that each man had the nutrients necessary to carry him through the day. The cost of the daily ration was set by BuSandA and it was this amount that formed the income side of the ledger. In 1944 the amount was $1.20, then by 1956 the amount per ration had increased to $1.32 for submarines. The Navy gave a higher amount of money to submarine rations in recognition of the hazardous duty performed by them. The Navy's current amount per submarine ration is about $7.80.

Not all submariners got a government paid ration. Some had and some continue to draw comrats or commuted rations. This meant that certain men drew the actual dollar amount in pay, but had to feed themselves.

In addition to the above described records the cook kept a Provisions Ledger, a Mess Control Sheet, and a set of records that pertained to his buy-outs. The system provided for drawing the basic food stocks from a tender which acted as a distribution point for BuSandA. In addition, the cook had the freedom to buy special items from civilian vendors who were listed in a local registry of approved and reputable suppliers. Of course, the paper work was additional as well. Requisitions, dockside inspections for quantity and quality of goods purchased and accounting records of such expenditures formed a separate set of records.

Since storage was such a huge problem in a submarine it was difficult for the cook to know exactly where all the food was hidden. Bilges, outboard of torpedoes and engines, shower stalls and decks were all used as storage space. This meant that taking inventory was a real challenge. Here was a case in point of the friction that sometimes appeared between the supply officers residing in ample spaces on tenders and submarine line officers who knew first hand just how hard it was to keep track of stored food. The supply types wanted tidy forms and accurate records reflecting amounts on hand, and amounts expended. The periodic inventory was a real sticking point. Submarines just didn't lend themselves to the shelving necessary for tight inventory control. Fortunately, most supply officers were sympathetic to the difficulties and rolled with the punches. How they managed to create a tight system out of the chaos of submarine commissary was always a mystery to submarine line officers.

One aspect of the commissary record keeping ordeal was given short shrift. This was the Navy's penchant to record all food that was wasted. It fought waste as best it could and to do so it demanded of submarine cooks an array of records and signatures that gave command approval for tossing away food. Spoilage and infestation were the major culprits requiring food surveys, but in submarines there was a third and more important contributor to food waste. It was the crew which tolerated only the best in quality. Food brought aboard which did not measure up to the crew's standards was not eaten. By necessity it was discharged to sea, usually through the garbage ejector or when in sufficient quantity through the torpedo tubes.

In such cases the cook had the choice of either paying for the wasted food from the daily ration or of attempting to regain the affected money loss through BuSandA's system of food survey. This took several more detailed forms with accompanying signatures. It was a burden beyond the cook's normal record keeping and it should come as no surprise that submarines had hardly any waste, at least as far as BuSandA was concerned.

There was lots of arithmetic in the cook's job. He needed it in determining how much food to buy, how to convert the Standard Navy Recipes and how to fill in the multitude of blank columns in the many records BuSandA demanded of him. The submarine commissary officer was of no help, since he was usually just out of submarine school. The best to be expected of a commissary officer was that he might stay out of the galley and off the back of those who struggled to put food on the mess tables and satisfy the supply types on the tender.

A prior chapter described food acquisition, storage and preparation on a modern nuclear ballistic missile submarine. A comparison of the same basic food service functions in the nineteen fifties and at the time of this publication points to how the computer has lifted much of the record-keeping burden from the shoulders of the submarine cook.

MENU DEVELOPMENT OVER THE YEARS

The following pages are the actual menus as described as well as two pages from a Navy Cook Book.

Page 79   The submarine menu originated from a hand written copy. This example is from the early fifties. Note the corrections by the lead cook for Monday's meat.

Page 81   A submarine menu from the Second World War proudly announces "fresh milk". The boat was either in port or on its first weeks of a patrol.

Page 83   The USS Cabazon's 1950 menu is typical of a submarine's food service during weekly operations.

Page 85   A 1999 menu for the USS Ashville shows the 50 year improvements of a submarine's menu. The crew's mess has a name and calorie and fat intakes are listed. Notice the double meat entrees for most meals.

Page 87   The USS Tunny's 1962 Christmas dinner menu was decorated and printed for all hands. Dependents were often invited to Christmas dinner for the duty section.

Page 89   Two pages from the US Navy Cookbook for 1920. The family size recipe for Roast Beef and Braised Beef can be found in Chapter 7.

NAV. S. and A. Form No. 133
(Revised July 1940)

BILL OF FARE FOR THE GENERAL MESS

U.S.S. _____

Week beginning ___12-1-48___, 19__

	BREAKFAST	DINNER	SUPPER
MONDAY	FRESH MILK FRESH FRUIT BOILED OATMEAL EGGS TO ORDER CRISP BACON DOUGHNUTS B.B.C.	CREAMED VEAL POTATOES BUTTERED GREEN BEANS TOAST----CELERY STICK ICED VANILLA CAKE FRESH MILK B.B.C.	RARE ROAST RIB OF BEEF NATURAL GRAVY CREAM WHIPPED POTATOES BUTTERED W.K. CORN F.F. FRESH MILK---VEG. SALAD ICE CREAM B.B.C.
TUESDAY	FRESH MILK FRESH FRUIT JUICE DRY CEREAL GRIDDLE CAKES PORK SAUSAGE SYRUP AND JAM B.B.C.	SALISBURY STEAK FRENCH FRIED POTATOES BUTTERED PEAS F.F. RICE PUDDING AND AVOSET FRESH MILK VEG. SALAD B.B.C.	MARYLAND FRIED CHICKEN SNOW FLAKED POTATOES BUTTERED ASPARAGUS GIBLET GRAVY GREEN SALAD FRESH MILK BLUEBERRY PIE F.F B.B.C.
WEDNESDAY	FRESH FRUIT CHILLED FRUIT JUICE CREAMED MINCED BEEF HOME FRIED POTATOES HOT COCOA DRY TOAST B.B.C.	GRILLED BEEF LIVERS FRIED BACON LYONNAISED POTATOES BUTTERED BRUSSEL SPROUTS ICED ORANGE JUICE ICED Banana Cake VEG. SALAD B.B.C.	ROAST LOIN OF PORK BOILED POTATOES NATURAL GRAVY CREAMED WAX BEANS APPLE PIE AND CHEESE COLESLAW CHILLED PUNCH B.B.C.
THURSDAY	FRESH FRUIT COLD ORANGE JUICE F.F. SCRAMBLED EGGS CRISP BACON GOGGLE EYES B.B.C.	BOILED FRANKS IN SPANISH SAUCE BOILED POTATOES SAUERKRAUT AND PORK BUTTERED LIMA BEANS F.F. FRUIT JELLO----COOKIES VEG. SALAD B.B.C.	GRILLED TENDERLOIN STEAK FRENCH FRIED POTATOES BUTTERED CORN INNER CIRCLE CAKE ICED LEMONADE VEG. SALAD B.B.C.
FRIDAY	FRESH FRUIT CHILLED GRAPEFRUIT JUICE BAKED BEANS WITH BACON STRIPS BOILED SOFT AND HARD EGGS B.B.C.	FRIED SCALLOPS TARTAR SAUCE SCALLOPED POTATOES BUTTERED CARROT STRIPS SLICED DILL PICKLES STRAWBERRY SHORTCAKE FRESH MILK	STUFFED BELL PEPPERS TOMATOE SAUCE MACORONI AND CHEESE BUTTERED STRING BEANS GREEN SALAD ICE CREAM B.B.C.
SATURDAY	FRESH MILK DRY CEREAL FRESH FRUIT FRENCH TOAST SLICED HAM MAPLE SYRUP DOUGHNUTS B.B.C.	POT ROAST OF BEEF BOILED POTATOES BOILED CABBAGE VEG. GRAVY SLICED PICKLE AND OLIVES ICE CREAM FRESH MILK B.B.C.	GRILLED HAM STEAKS PAN ROASTED POTATOES BUTTERED BROCCOLI BROWN GRAVY ICED CHOCOLATE CAKE GREEN SALAD FRESH MILK B.B.C.
SUNDAY	FRESH MILK FRESH FRUIT DRY CEREAL EGGS TO ORDER BREAKFAST STEAKS FRENCH FRIED POTATOES B.B.C.	ROAST CHICKEN BREAD DRESSING CREAMED WHIPPED POTATOES GIBLET GRAVY BUTTERED CRANBERRY SAUCE AND OLIVES VEG. SALAD	

U.S.S. CABEZON SS334

Week beginning 16 January, 1950

	BREAKFAST	DINNER	SUPPER
MONDAY	Fresh Milk Cereal Creamed Beef Fried Potatoes Toast Danish Rolls Chilled Juice BB&C	Breaded Veal Cutlets Mashed Potatoes Asparagus Salad Brown Gravy Dessert BB&C	Swiss Steaks Oven Brown Potatoes Green Beans Salad Brown Gravy Dessert BB&C
TUESDAY	Fresh Milk Cereal French Toast Fried Ham Donuts Chilled Juice BB&C	Grilled Pork Chops Mashed Potatoes Cauliflower F. F. Salad Pork Gravy Salad Dessert BB&C	Sweet & Sour Spare Ribs Boiled Potatoes Brussel Sprouts Salad Bar-B-Q Sauce Dessert BB&C
WEDNESDAY	Fresh Milk Cereal Scrambled Eggs Fried Bacon Cinnamon Rolls Chilled Juice BB&C	Virginia Baked Ham Mashed Sweet Potatoes Green Peas Salad Raisen Sauce Pickles & Olives Mustard & Catsup Dessert BB&C	Pot Roast of Beef Oven Brown Potatoes Peas & Carrots Salad Natural Gravy Dessert BB&C
THURSDAY	Fresh Milk Cereal Minced Beef Fried Potatoes Toast Danish Rolls Chilled Juice BB&C	Grilled Tenderloin Steaks French Fried Potatoes Golden Sweet Corn Salad Steak Sauces Dessert BB&C	Grilled Ham Steaks Diced Fried Potatoes Boiled Fresh Carrots Salad Mustard & Catsup Pickles & Olives Dessert BB&C
FRIDAY	Fresh Milk Cereal Hot Griddle Cakes Fried Bacon Cinnamon Rolls Chilled Juice BB&C	Fried Salmon Steaks Potatoes Au-gratin Lima Beans Tarter Sauce Salad Dessert BB&C	Steak en Casserole Baked Potatoes Succotash Salad Natural Gravy Dessert BB&C
SATURDAY	Fresh Milk Cereal Corned Beef Hash Soft & Hard Eggs Donuts Chilled Juice BB&C	Boiled Corned Beef Boiled Potatoes Boiled Cabbage Boiled Carrots Mustard & Catsup Pickles & Olives Dessert BB&C	Grilled Hamburgers Fried Potatoes Golden Sweet Corn Salad Sliced Onions Lettuce, Tomatoes Dessert BB&C
SUNDAY	Fresh Milk Cereal Eggs to Order Minute Steaks Toast Danish Rolls Chilled Juice BB&C	Roast Tom Turkey Mashed Potatoes Creamed Peas Salad Giblet Gravy Sage Dressing Dessert BB&C	Cold Cuts of Meats Cold Potatoes Salad Cold Baked Beans Sliced Cheese Sliced Tomatoes Leaf Lettuce Dessert BB&C

APPROVED: Respectfully submitted,

USS Asheville (SSN 758) IMPORT WEEK 1

Da Kine Menu

"The SUBROCK Café" NEY 2000 & 2001 Silver Medallist

Keep your eyes on th

healthier items that are highlighted with a ✓. These are some of the better items to eat!!

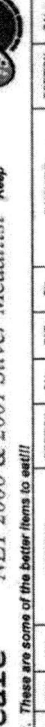

	BREAKFAST	PORTION SIZE	CAL	FAT (g)	CH (mg)	LUNCH	PORTION SIZE	CAL	FAT (g)	CH (mg)	DINNER	PORTION SIZE	CAL	FAT (g)	CH (mg)
M O N D A Y	✓ ORANGE & ASST. JUICES ✓ CHILLED FRESH FRUIT ASST. EGGS TO ORDER PANCAKES W/ SYRUP ✓ ASST. READY TO EAT CEREAL OVEN FRIED BACON GRILLED HAM SLICES ✓ HASH BROWN POTATOES FRUIT KOLACHES	4 OZ ½ CUP 1 EGG 2 EA A/L 2 SLICES 1 SLICE ½ CUP 1 EA	53 70 90 246 86 262 165 85 165	0 0 7 6 8 10 7 0 6	0 0 213 64 13 50 50 0 22	TOMATO BISQCUE KALUA PIG SANDWICH ✓ HULI HULI CHICKEN TASTY ONION RINGS ✓ STEAMED RICE ✓ CINNAMON GLAZED CARROTS ✓ SUBROCK SALAD BAR CONGO BARS	1 CUP 1 EA 2½/2 OZ ½ CUP ½ CUP ½ CUP 1 SQ	122 453 298 234 181 78 13 257	5 25 10 5 0 2 0 12	0 111 75 0 0 10 0 50	NAVY BEAN SOUP OVEN ROASTED BEEF ✓ BAKED TUNA STEAKS W/ PINEAPPLE SALSA ✓ MASHED POTATOES RICH BROWN GRAVY ✓ SPRING PEAS W/ ONIONS ✓ SUBROCK SALAD BAR HOT FRENCH BREAD ICED YELLOW CAKE	1 CUP 2 SLICES 4 OZ ½ CUP ¼ CUP ½ CUP ¾ CUP 1 EA 1 SQ	116 475 211 96 78 75 13 161 202	1 37 13 2 6 2 0 1 8	0 124 59 5 9 0 0 0 39
T U E S D A Y	✓ ORANGE & ASST. JUICES ✓ CHILLED FRESH FRUIT ASST. EGGS TO ORDER CINNAMON FRENCH TOAST ✓ ASST. READY TO EAT CEREAL OVEN FRIED BACON CREAMED BEEF ✓ HASH BROWN POTATOES PEACH COFFEE CAKE	4 OZ ½ CUP 1 EGG 2 SLICES A/L 2 SLICES ⅔ CUP ½ CUP 1 PIECE	53 70 90 182 86 226 165 85 232	0 0 7 14 8 11 7 0 8	0 0 213 52 13 150 54 0 39	✓ CHICKEN NOODLE SOUP SPICY BEEF SUB ✓ BAKED HALIBUT STEAKS W/ GARLIC CAPERS SAUCE FRENCH FRIED POTATOES ✓ STEAMED MIXED VEGETABLES ✓ SUBROCK SALAD BAR CHOCOLATE BROWNIES	1 CUP 1 EA 4 OZ ¾ CUP ½ CUP ½ CUP ½ CUP 1 SQ	58 413 226 390 161 70 13 361	1 6 15 21 0 0 0 19	0 24 64 0 0 0 0 68	✓ CREAM OF TOMATO SOUP OVEN ROASTED TURKEY W/ CRANBERRY SAUCE ✓ SNOWFLUXE POTATOES GIBLET GRAVY ✓ GARDEN GREEN BEANS ✓ SUBROCK SALAD BAR HOT DINNER ROLLS PUMPKIN PIE W/ TOPPING	1 CUP 4 OZ ¾ CUP ¼ CUP ½ CUP 1 CUP 2 EA 1 SLICE	98 342 92 85 68 13 302 243	2 7 6 2 0 0 10 10	0 108 5 0 46 0 0 64
W E D N E S D A Y	✓ ORANGE & ASST. JUICES ✓ CHILLED FRESH FRUIT ASST. EGGS TO ORDER HOT WAFFLES W/ SYRUP ✓ ASST. READY TO EAT CEREAL OVEN FRIED BACON BREAKFAST SAUSAGE ✓ HASH BROWN POTATOES ICED SNAILS	4 OZ ½ CUP 1 EGG 1 EA A/L 2 EA 1 SLICE ½ CUP 1 EA	53 70 90 182 86 161 165 85 165	0 0 7 14 8 6 7 0 6	0 0 213 49 13 54 50 0 22	NEW ENGLAND CLAM CHOWDER SUBROCK BRISKET ✓ TUNA FISH SANDWICH POTATO CHIPS ✓ SQUASH RATATOURI ✓ MACARONI SALAD ✓ SUBROCK RELISH TRAY CRISP TOFFEE BARS	1 CUP 1 EA 1 EA ⅔ CUP ⅔ CUP 1 CUP 2 EA 2 SQ	218 512 350 190 79 151 129 246	10 4 12 10 0 5 1 15	41 25 40 0 0 24 0 25	✓ CHICKEN BARLEY SOUP TEXMEX CHILI SPICY BURRITOS ✓ SPANISH RICE CHEESEY REFRIED BEANS ✓ CALICO CORN ✓ SUBROCK SALAD BAR ✓ WARMED TORTILLAS BLUEBERRY CRUNCH	1 CUP 1 CUP 2 EA ¾ CUP ¾ CUP 1 CUP 1 CUP 2 EA 1 SLICE	81 291 462 207 129 74 13 232 213	1 15 5 5 2 2 0 1 8	0 54 112 0 14 0 0 0 50
T H U R S D A Y	✓ ORANGE & ASST. JUICES ✓ CHILLED FRESH FRUIT ASST. EGGS TO ORDER PANCAKES W/ SYRUP ✓ ASST. READY TO EAT CEREAL OVEN FRIED BACON CORNED BEEF HASH ✓ HASH BROWN POTATOES APPLE TURNOVERS	4 OZ ½ CUP 1 EGG 2 EA A/L 2 EA ⅔ CUP ½ CUP 1 EA	53 70 90 182 86 161 165 85 165	0 0 7 14 8 6 7 0 6	0 0 213 64 13 54 50 0 22	PORTABELLO MUSHROOM SOUP SPAGHETTI W/ MEAT BALLS GRILLED ITALIAN SAUSAGE ✓ STEAMED ASPARAGUS ✓ SIMMERED CAULIFLOWER ✓ SUBROCK SALAD BAR HOT GARLIC BITES GINGERBREAD W/ TOPPING	1 CUP 3 MTBAL 1 EA ½ CUP ½ CUP 1 CUP 2 EA 1 SQ	127 520 201 16 30 13 277 210	9 16 14 0 0 0 13 8	2 67 49 0 0 0 34 28	FRENCH ONION SOUP BOARDWALK CHICKEN BAKED HAM STEAKS ✓ HERBED SAFFRON RICE ✓ STEAMED BROCCOLI COMBO ✓ SUBROCK SALAD BAR HOT CLOVER LEAF ROLLS COCONUT CREAM PIE	1 CUP 2 PIECE 1 SLICE ¾ CUP ¾ CUP ¾ CUP 2 ROLLS 1 SLICE	108 364 202 193 56 13 302 315	9 15 10 0 0 0 10 17	0 108 59 0 0 0 0 73

85

U.S.S. TUNY (SSG-282)

Pearl Harbor, Hawaii

D. STAHL, LCDR
Commanding Officer
J. A. BURGESS, LT.
Executive Officer
G. J. PATTEN, LT.
Operations Officer
F. H. INGRAM, LT.
Engineering Officer
J. L. CORKILL, LTJG
Communications Officer
J. G. SHAFFER, LTJG
Music Officer
W. A. HARDT, LTJG
Guidance Officer
L. A. WOMACK, LTJG
Supply and Commissary Officer
P. A. BEEM, LTJG
Ordnance Officer
W. J. DONALDSON, ENS
Assistant Engineer
E. W. WINEBERG, ENCM(SS)
Chief Of The Boat

COMMISSARY DIVISION

W. T. PRESS, CSC(SS)   L. C. HAMMOCK, CS1(SS)

MAYO, CS1   D. N. FATE CS1(SS)

Christmas Dinner
1962

V-8 Cocktail   Shrimp Cocktail
Cream of Tomato Soup

Baked Hawaii Ham   Roast Young Tom
Pineapple Sauce   Giblet Gravy
Fried Pineapple Ring   Bread Dressing
Candied Sweet Potatoes   Mashed Potatoes
Buttered Broccoli   Creamed Peas

Celery Stalks   Carrot Sticks   Cucumber Slices
Waldorf Salad   Combination Salad

Fruit Cake   Pumpkin Pie
Shelled Nuts   Hard Candy
Ice Cream   Brown and Serve Rolls
Coffee   Butter   Milk

MEATS

ROAST BEEF

Cut 80 pounds ribs of beef into 6-pound pieces; wipe dry. Place in roasting pans and rub in as much flour all over as the meat will hold, letting a little of the flour drop over the bottom of the pan. Place dots of drippings over the top of the roast, using about 4 tablespoonfuls in all. Place pan in the oven and let alone for 25 minutes or until browned nicely. Then draw out the pan and pour in about 2 cupfuls of boiling water. Baste the meat all over, place back in the oven and close drafts, reducing the temperature of the oven to a very moderate heat. Baste every 10 or 15 minutes. When nearly done season with salt and pepper; baste again. You cannot baste the meat too often. Figure about 13 minutes to the pound to cook the meat. The first intense heat of the oven sears the meat, retaining the juices. Reducing the heat cooks the inside without further scorching the surface.

When meat is done, remove from pan. Set pan on top of the range, add a little hot water and stir well to detach all the particles of flour that have adhered to the pan. Boil and stir for 4 or 5 minutes, then strain into a gravy dish. Skim off all fat which you keep for drippings.

The practice of adding flour to the roasting pan, to burn and thicken the gravy, and with burned, bitter tasting sugar, should be discouraged. No more thickening is really required than the stray particles of flour which fell from the meat when first started to roast. These have cooked well and browned during the time of roasting.

BRAISED BEEF

56 lbs. beef
2 lbs. salt pork
2 lbs. carrots
2 lbs. turnips
Flour
4 bay-leaves
12 cloves
Celery tops
8 lbs. onions

The kind of meat best for this purpose is round, vein and shoulder-clods. Cut the fat pork 3 inches long and ½ inch square; dice the vegetables. Cut the meat in about 8-pound pieces, take a steel and punch a hole parallel with the grain of the meat and insert one of the lardons of pork, continue this until all the pork is used. Place a baking pan on top of the range, put remaining scraps of salt pork together with some beef drippings in the bottom of the pan, allow to become hot, then add the beef which has been previously well dredged with flour, allow to become well browned, then add the diced vegetables and cook for 20 minutes, then add the stock or water to fill the pan, invert another pan to prevent escape of steam and finish cooking in the oven, turning the basting the meat frequently; this process of braising may be carried out in the same manner by using the steam coppers. Remove the fat from the liquid, strain, season and serve.

BOILED BEEF

70 lbs. beef
2 lbs. onions
2 lbs. turnips
2 lbs. carrots

Cut the beef in 8-pound pieces, place in boiling water, allow it to boil hard for 5 minutes, then reduce

CHAPTER 13
REGIONAL AND FOREIGN DISHES

Many dishes served aboard submarines were distinctly regional. Those boats stationed in Norfolk, Charleston and Key West had many dishes that reflected southern eating habits. Chicken Jambalaya, black eyed peas, grits, fritters, fried okra and collard greens were to be found on menus. Southern fried chicken had lost its regional appeal and had become a national favorite by the time the Second World War was a fact.

The New England Boiled Dinner could be found on menus, but mostly so on the New London boats. Southwest cuisine with its hot flavors had not made the submarine menus in the 50s and 60s, but traditional Mexican dishes were often served. Enchiladas were occasionally on the menu as was Mexican fried rice. Chili con Carne was served as a type of stew.

Italian dishes and even whole meals were a favorite of the crew. Spaghetti, lasagna, and chicken or beef parmesan with garlic toast were special occasions on submarines. Wine was to be seen served during these meals on rare and unofficial (not to mention illegal) occasions.

Some cooks were able to serve Chinese dishes including Egg Foo Yong and Chop Suey. Even though most of the regional and foreign dishes could be found in the Standard Navy Recipe Service it took a dedicated cook to put such a meal together. There's no doubt that these dishes required a delicate touch.

Curried meat dishes could be said to have come from India, but the reality was that such dishes were thoroughly Americanized. It wasn't a good idea for a submarine cook to go too far out on an experimental limb when preparing regional and foreign dishes. The crew liked what it knew and this meant steaks and hamburgers being only occasionally punctuated by foreign and regional dishes.

CHARLES BROWN'S CHILI CON CARNE (J-30)

This recipe is modern in the sense that recipes from the southwest and those that are highly seasoned with chili peppers are currently in the van of Epicurean favorites. Many restaurants have opened that feature these types of dishes and when the eyes water from "caliente" the cook is judged to be a success. Submarines along with other ships served chili con carne with reservation. It is now a subject for contests and cook-offs. Here is Charles Brown's version that that he made while on the boats. It exploits the relation of beans to the meat and serves about six people.

Ingredients	Measure/Weight	Method
Beans, kidney, dry	1 pound	Soak the beans overnight, remove any foreign matter and cook until the beans are soft.
Beef, boneless,	3/4 pound	Brown the beef, drain off excess ground fat.
Onions, chopped	1 large	Sauté onions, green peppers and garlic in 1 tbsp oil for about 10 minutes.
Peppers, green, chopped	2 small	
Garlic, finely chopped	1 large clove	
Tomatoes, canned	1 med can	
Tomato paste	1 small can	
Water, hot	1 and 1/2 cup	
Chili powder	1/4 tsp	
Salt	pinch	
Pepper, cayenne	pinch	
Sugar	2 tbsp	Combine beef, onion, garlic and peppers into tomato mixture. Add salt, cayenne pepper, chili powder and sugar with beans. Mix well. Bring to a boil, reduce heat and simmer about 2 hours.

The above recipe will provide a hearty meal for a big family, however, Charles sometimes modifies the recipe as follows:
"Increase the amount of kidney beans by one half. Pour one half of the soft beans into a blender, add a small amount of water and blend into a soup. Mix this heavy syrup with the other ingredients. One may also use pinto beans for a dark, rich color. The result is a richer and tastier version of the Navy recipe."

CHARLES BROWN'S SHRIMP EGG FOO YONG

This recipe is not found in the Navy Recipe Service. Of the foreign food favorites Chinese ranked behind Mexican and Italian. A few submarine cooks were able to put out a real Chinese meal with chop suey, sweet and sour pork and Won Ton soup. When a Chinese meal was prepared it was normally while the boat was in port. The complications of Chinese food preparation were more than most submarine cooks could overcome while rolling and tossing on the surface or fighting the snorkel. The following will be enough to make six mini-omelets.

Ingredients	Measure/Weight	Method
Make egg foo yong sauce:		
Oyster flavor sauce	2 tbsp	
Soy sauce	2 tsp	
Sugar	1 tsp	
Cornstarch	1 tsp	Combine the ingredients by Soup stock (any)
White pepper	dash	whipping with a wisk. Warm
	1/4 cup	when ready to serve.
Make egg foo yong:		
Eggs	5	
Shrimp, baby	12	
Scallion, chopped	6	
Bean sprouts	Two pinches per mini-omelet	Whip the eggs and season with salt, white pepper, soy sauce and sesame seed oil. Chop shrimp
Salt	pinch	and scallion finely. Add and mix oil
Pepper, white	pinch	to whipped egg. Divide and pour
Sesame seed oil	6 dashes	into greased muffin pan with six muffin pits. Bake in oven at low heat until done (about ten minutes). Remove omelets from muffin pan and cover with warm sauce. Top with finely chopped parsley.

This dish will go well with fried or steamed rice. Increase the ingredients for larger omelets.

JIM MAYO'S HAWAIIAN SPARE RIBS

This is one of two dishes that Jim Mayo learned when he was apprenticing at the Royal Hawaiian Hotel while Tunny was in port after one of its grueling Northern Patrols. The hotel was eager to have submarine cooks learn its secrets for making sumptuous Hawaiian dishes.

Ingredients	Measure/Weight	Method
Spareribs	8 lbs	
Stock, chicken	1 cup	
Sauce, Soy	1/2 cup	
Vinegar, apple	1/2 cup	
Sugar, brown	1 and 1/2 cups	
Wine, white	1/2 cup	
Pineapple, canned, chunks in juice	2 cups	
Pineapple, crushed	1 cup	Combine chicken stock, soy sauce, white wine, vinegar, brown sugar, pineapple chunks, and crushed pineapple in pan and bring to a boil.
Peppers, green diced into 1/2 cubes	1/4 cup	
Garlic, chopped fine	2 tbsp	
Butter or olive oil	1 tbsp	
Cornstarch	3 and 1/2 tbsp	Reduce heat. Bring to slow simmer. Blend corn starch and cold water and add to liquid mixture, stirring to prevent lumping. Simmer until thick (about 3 minutes). Place onions, green peppers, garlic and butter in frying pan on medium heat. Saute until color begins to change to translucent. Add mixture to sauce.
Cold water	1/2 cup	
		Season ribs with salt and pepper. Place on grill or in oven, rib side down. Cook at 350 deg F for 45 to 50 minutes, turning once after 30 minutes. Remove from grill or oven and let stand for 20 minutes. Cut into portions. Place in deep baking pan and pour hot pineapple sauce over ribs. Cover and bake at 300 deg F for about 2 hours, or until tender.

This recipe is equally applied to either pork or beef ribs. The cooking time for pork is normally slightly less than for beef.

The baking times noted are for regular ribs. The sauce can be used for chicken. Serves about 8 people and is normally accompanied by steamed rice served on a separate dish.

JIM MAYO'S TERIYAKI STEAK

This recipe and the Hawaiian Sparerib recipe were both learned at the Royal Hawaiian Hotel. Jim submitted both recipes to the Navy Recipe Service which then integrated the recipes into its card system.

Ingredients	Measure/Weight	Method
Sauce, soy	2 and 1/2 cups	
Wine, white	1/2 cup	
Ginger root, fresh, chopped	1 tbsp	
Garlic, chopped	2 tbsp	
Sugar, granulated	1 and 1/2 cups	
Juice, orange	1 cup	Combine ingredients to make a sauce.
Steak, tenderloin	8 lbs.	Place beef sirloin or tenderloin steaks in plastic or glass container. Pour sauce over steaks and put in refrigerator for 1 to 6 hours depending on the toughness of the meat. Turn meat in sauce 2 or 3 times to insure good distribution. Remove beef from sauce and cook on grill. Baste meat with sauce as the meat cooks.

If one desires to keep the sauce for further use simmer the sauce for fifteen minutes to prevent cultivation of bacteria.

This is a marvelous beef for cubes on a skewer together with mushroom halves, green pepper quarters and onion sections.

The sauce is equally good for chicken or pork.

CHAPTER 14
POPULARITY VERSUS WASTE

Who could argue with the selection of eggs to order, bacon or sausage, hash browns and toast as the number one hit with submariners? This is what the men wanted more than any other breakfast meal. The cooks knocked themselves out to prepare the eggs exactly as each man demanded. The suspicion exists that the controversial ground and chipped beef breakfasts were so often found on the menu just to give the cooks a rest. It was very hard to foul up S.O.S. or Foreskins and their consistency was its best selling point. What you ate yesterday you could depend upon getting today.

After many personal interviews with submarine cooks SRC is convinced that submariners have had a love-hate relation with these two items since their inception, probably sometime during the Civil War. Modern submarines serve the same two dishes, get the same grumbling as fifty years ago and have no intention of ever doing anything different. After all, it's a Navy tradition and that alone makes the dishes worthwhile.

Interestingly, most of the grumbling comes from the younger submariners. They have not eaten the Navy's traditional breakfast long enough to develop a taste for the items. The old hands dig into the meal, pitching the dripping hunks of toast into their mouths with gusto. It seems to be an acquired taste.

In so far as this study is concerned, the recipes for both items are to be found in the breakfast section, (Chapter 5) as numbers one and two in popularity. SRC is convinced that if there is one item most missed on the home breakfast table it is one of the two. Our hope is that submariners will be able to enjoy these two dishes by closing their eyes and pretending that they are once again in the after battery.

The second controversial food item was Spam. Hormel made Spam during the Second World War to use up otherwise-wasted shoulder cuts from hogs. It became the laughing stock of movies and gained a reputation as the food least liked by the military. Actually, our study showed that the men in submarines didn't mind Spam. It could be turned into several palatable dishes and it could be efficiently stored in submarines. Its shelf life was about a thousand years so it was tolerated with ease at the end of each patrol.

The other two meals of the day had their favorite dishes and their least liked ones. Without doubt special mention must be made of liver. It matters not whether the liver comes from veal or beef. The very idea of liver to most submariners is revolting. While liver occupies the distinction of being the least liked item on the noon and evening meal menus it deserves the recognition that the few men who liked liver, really liked it. Sometimes the cook would prepare a few servings of liver for those who enjoyed the dish.

During the fifties BuSandA responded to the gripes of destroyer sailors. They claimed that all the good cuts of beef went to submarines and they were stuck with shoulders and knuckles. The Navy took aggressive action and demanded that all ships, and particularly submarines, had to buy "units" of beef. A unit was essentially a half of a cow cut down the middle. With the choice cuts came all the lower cuts which, of course, included liver. This and other hunks of less desirable beef got shot out the torpedo tubes or garbage ejectors with regularity. The Navy could force submarines to buy the junk, but it couldn't make us eat it.

The worst quality beef came from Britain. This would have not presented a problem to the United States Navy were it not for the fact that so many of our submarines spent so much time either in Holy Loch or Portsmouth. NAFI, the British Navy's supply system, bought all of its beef from Argentina. Eating so much mutton, the British sailor wasn't very discriminating about beef. It didn't take long for our boats to find out that British beef was inedible. Our Guppies fried, broiled, and boiled the meat. We tried it first as steaks which were a disaster. The long walks from Patagonia to Buenos Aires turned muscle into gristle. The meat was untenable, no matter how it was prepared. The best use of the beef was to flavor a stew, but the meat then had to be removed because the men might accidentally swallow a piece and wind up unfit for duty. Once again, the torpedomen got practice and the killer whales of the North got fat.

The following is a list of the least liked dishes for the noon and evening meals. They are not listed in any particular order. The reader may disagree with many dishes on the list, but the least-like items include:

 Corned beef
 Rabbit
 Fish
 Hot dogs
 Corned beef and cabbage
 Sloppy Joes
 Stuffed peppers
 Processed meat called Horsecock
 Hard boiled eggs
 Cabbage
 Turkey ala King
 Grits
 Goulash
 Swiss Steak
 Lamb

It should be noted that lamb was very seldom prepared in submarines because of its odor when cooking. Occasionally, lamb could be found on menus when the boat was in port and rigged for surface with all hatches open.

There were a few food items that got aboard submarines that were refused by the crews out of hand. During President Kennedy's administration the Navy decided that its sailors were flabby. It instituted a physical fitness program. Directives filtered down to submarines, but nobody put much stock in the idea. While it was true that most submariners were in deplorable physical condition it was regarded as a job related disability. The Navy sent cases of Metrical to every submarine. They arrived on deck without the need for a requisition. This thick goo was supposed to replace meals. The idea of giving up a meal for anything, much less that of a sweet syrup in a can was intolerable to every self respecting submariner. The cans went over the side as soon as the submarine passed the one hundred fathom curve. One captain refused to let any crew member touch the offensive little cans in their crates. He simply left them where they had been delivered and dove out from under them.

Strangely, the Navy had a penchant for buying inferior rice. BuSandA prided itself on inspecting foods to be purchased, but it often failed to somehow test batches of rice. What made some of it inedible no one seemed to know, but when an inferior bag of it came aboard it only took one meal to survey the rest of the bag into the garbage ejector.

Submarine cooks and commissary officers hated to waste food. They put their energies into buying what the men liked and tried to limit the food to be surveyed. The major reason for this frugal concern was not the health of the men, but the paper work involved in a food survey. While it was possible to dump food because of spoilage etc. and to regain from BuSandA the money expended, most cooks and commissary officers elected to simply dump the unwanted food and accept the loss on the submarine's records.

When underway in transit waste was commonly dumped over the side by breaking rig for dive, opening the after battery hatch and sending a mess cook topside with the bags of waste. This was a break from his duties. He was able to smell fresh air and to look at the world outside of the after battery. When submerged and when on special operations the garbage ejector was used. This was located on the starboard side just aft of the scullery on Guppy submarines. It was for all practical purposes a small torpedo tube with breach and muzzle doors. Since it was a potential hazard to the boat's water tight integrity only qualified petty officers were allowed to use it. Plastic mesh bags were stuffed with refuse and weighted down with spent bullets. They were slid into the ejector and water pressure shot them out into the sea to hopefully sink to the bottom.

Submariners have always been and continue to be the best fed sailors in the Navy. Cooks, now called Culinary Specialists, deserve very high marks for the quality of their meals. There was and is little that submarine sailors don't eat and won't tolerate, because those items never appear on the menu.

CHAPTER 15
A SINGLE FISH DISH

During the Second World War fish was not often served aboard submarines. This tradition carried over into the Cold War until advances in food preservation made it possible to store frozen fish for prolonged periods. Even in the best of conditions submarine crews wanted red meat in favor of fish. The men tolerated poultry, but fish was served only occasionally.

During the 1950s and 60s boats on Atlantic northern runs stopped off at Portsmouth, England to replenish food supplies before heading up the Irish Sea. The British Navy's supply system, NAFI, carried a variety of fresh frozen fish that was not available in the United States. On these trips boats would often stock frozen Scottish trout. The crews thought the fish was delicious and marveled at why they weren't getting fish on a regular schedule. But once back home in American ports they slipped back into their red meat preferences and fish once again became a rarity on the menu.

Holy Loch nuclear boats experienced the same pleasant surprise. Scotland and Britain had a lot of wonderful foods not eaten in America.

The exceptions to avoidance of fish were canned tuna and frozen shrimp, both of which were served in variety. Tuna was normally mixed with noodles or vegetables in casseroles. Shrimp was used in Chinese dishes or curried into casseroles. On occasion a boat would buy frozen Bangladesh scampi. These were huge shrimp that came in a block of ice. They were made into fried scampi, but because of the coast (nearly that of lobster) they were served only in port to the duty section of the crew.

Salmon was another exception and was inexpensive. This was served normally while in port and was normally baked. Salmon could also be combined with finely chopped vegetables and spice to make patties which were fried.

Some fish on the normal market never made it onto the submarine menus because they were too "fishy" for most submariners' taste. Shellfish including oysters and scallops were only to be found in soup and even then the oysters were canned.

We offer in this volume only one fish recipe, Salmon Croquettes, which were considered by submarine crews to be a delicacy and which could be prepared using either fresh or canned salmon.

GEORGE, "BART" LOCKWOOD'S SALMON CROQUETTES (H-10)

This is a recipe from the Navy Standard Recipe Service geared down to family size. George served from 1959 to 1969 on the Clamagore (SS-343), qualified on the Chivo (SS-341), then served on the Rasher (SSR-269), the Threadfin (SS-410) and the Sea Poacher (SS-406). He was a first class torpedoman and a daily customer of all those cooks in all those boats. Now it is George's time to cook for all his shipmates. In fairness, it should be noted that his wife, Lynn had an active hand in preparing the following recipe for four, two patties each. The Navy's recipe called for deep fat frying. Lynn suggests an alternative. Also, canned salmon is now largely replaced by salmon in a pouch. This eliminates the need for bone watching.

Ingredients	Measure/Weight	Method
Salmon, in pouch	2 7.1 ounce pouches	Place salmon and liquid in mixing bowl.
Crumb, cracker	1/2 cup	
Salt	1/4 tsp	
Pepper	1/4 tsp	
Onions, minced	1/4 cup	
Celery seed	1/8 tsp	
Lemon juice	1 tbsp	Flake salmon with fork. Add the beaten egg, cracker crumbs, parsley, salt, pepper, celery seed, and lemon juice. Mix ingredients and shape into eight patties.
Egg, large	1	
Parsley, chopped	1/2 tsp	
Oil, canola	2 tbsp	Heat in frying pan. Place patties in pan and fry until browned, about 3 to 4 minutes per side.
Lemon wedges	8	Slice and set aside.
Prepare Dill Sauce:		
Mayonnaise	1/2 cup	
Lemon juice	2 tbsp	
Dill weed, dry	1/2 tsp	
Pepper	1/4 tsp	
Hot sauce	1/2 tsp	Mix together thoroughly. Spread over patties if serving on bun. If not, place on platter in small bowl with lemon wedges.

Serve as an entrée with vegetables or as sandwich in a bun. Dill mixture can be used either way.

CHAPTER 16
TABLE ETIQUETTE

There are probably three levels of training for proper and civilized eating habits in submarines. At the highest level of development is the United States Naval Academy. This institution turns boys into gentlemen and officers. As a plebe the young men are put through their paces academically, physically and socially. They quickly learn table manners not so much from books as the immediate and terrifying expectations of older and more mature students. They eat, sleep and study at attention. They quickly learn what utensil goes where and when it is used. Throughout this early phase of education the Academy student is familiarized with the need for politeness and the absolute necessity to eat everything on his or her plate. At the meal table they speak when spoken to by older students who ask them to recite various nonsense relating distantly to the Navy. The memorized words flow from mouths that are required to be vacant of food during speech. The thirty minute eating time is largely devoted to harassing the plebes and the actual amount of food consumed by them is correspondingly reduced. There is no need of dieting at the Academy. This is the custom now and it has been the same for the life of the institution.

Officer Candidate School in Newport, Rhode Island approached the subject from a different angle. Here, the student was a seaman apprentice. He ate off of trays pulled through serving lines like most enlisted men going through basic training. Because the curriculum, which was extensive, had to be covered in sixteen weeks there was little room for learning the "gentleman" side of being an officer. Never the less, the Navy knew its priorities and one subject was called, "Naval Orientation". Contained therein were all the rules for being civilized according to Navy rules. A part of this orientation pertained to the dinner table and how to be courteous and affable during the eating process. Unfortunately the only application of the know-how in the book was relevant to multiple choice answers on a weekly quiz.

No matter how a commissioned officer gained his knowledge of table etiquette he was expected to be reasonably versed in the finer points of eating in polite society. The wardroom was the testing ground of such knowledge and it was unforgiving. Should a newly minted officer make a mistake at the dinner table when the captain had expectations in this domain the poor man was likely to receive a substandard first fitness report.

The enlisted man went through basic training which, in so far as etiquette was concerned, could have been considered on-the-job training. While he may not have had any expectations of his fellow trainee in the beginning, certain unwritten rules began to develop. Each command and each ship added to the unwritten rules so that when he eventually found himself on a submarine the rules were already well entrenched. Still, the older men taught the younger ones the submarine rules. When a youngster thought he'd be salty by saying, "Sling me some bread," he was surprised that the bread was not forthcoming. The after battery was a training ground for these young men. They quickly learned that courtesy was a real and vibrant commodity in a submarine.

There were probably fewer places on earth where the words, "Excuse me," were more often used than in a submarine. Because of the close proximity of the men, courtesy and civility were and continue to be demanded in large doses. So often in the movies one sees and hears sweating and cursing sailors making what Hollywood thinks is submarine salty talk. Those who have not served in submarines would be amazed at just how polite these sweating and cursing sailors can be.

The crew's mess in a fleet type boat and Guppy was physically organized so that mess cooks arranged thirty or so settings at a time. This required a knowledge of where eating utensils were placed in relation to the plate. While butter knives were beyond a submarine's organizational necessity and mugs were used rather than cups and saucers, the basic arrangements were present. Serving plates and bowls were on each table (usually four tables, six to eight men to a table). This required each man to ask that a bowl or plate be passed. The word, "Please" accompanied such requests if the expectant eater desired the bowl to be passed to him. Manliness or macho in a submarine was established by competence on the job, not by bravado at the table.

The subject of civility and etiquette could not be complete without an explanation of profanity and the role it played in a submariner's social interactions. Profanity was an art that was learned over many years of gently abusing the English language and in developing an ear for cadence and rhythm. The true artist, normally only found in first class and chief petty officers who have honed the knife edge of profanity to a razor sharpness, was able to insert four letter words into sentences to give them flavor, texture and above all else, cadence. Those who were the real experts were able to dissect words in mid sentence and insert a swear word between syllables. Normally, swear words were adjectives or adverbs used to add emphasis to a subject or predicate. The appropriate matching of the swear word to the modified word took years of practice.

While profanity in submarines may not have been as pervasive as one might think, there were certain foods that deserve description using words that were in civilian life regarded as profane. Minced beef in tomato sauce on toast was S.O.S. The term did not refer to a ship in distress, but rather to the similarity of the mixture to excrement and the toast to a shingle. Its first cousin was chipped beef in a cream sauce over toast. This was simply referred to as foreskins. These derogatory descriptors did not at all mean a dislike of the dish. On the contrary, true sailors loved the two breakfast dishes as much as Navy beans.

There were many other profane titles for Navy foods, but the only other one popular enough to deserve attention here is luncheon meat, glazed, otherwise known as horsecock. The similarity of the meat product is too similar to what one might see on a farm to be ignored. A fourth place edible mixture that needs no further comment was tomato aspic.

Nothing was so obscene in a submarine as a young man who believed that he could show his maturity by throwing around profanity. It became a nuisance and irritant to those around him. Usually, an older sailor would have mercy on the young man and tell him to shut his mouth.

Profanity was also a matter of geography. While working in cramped spaces profanity helped to relieve the frustration that often accompanied these tough jobs. At the same time it was not easily tolerated in the crew's mess. For one thing, there wasn't much talking of any sort when the men had their mouths full of food. For another, what talk did exist had to conform to the standards of the older men. Business was a suitable subject. Submariners most often talked about their steel environment. Most of the conversation was done by the more senior petty officers. The young men listened and learned. Women was the most tempting subject, but as a dinner topic had to be reigned in to the most civil and general descriptions.

All in all, submarine enlisted men were not the dumb characters portrayed in movies. They were and are intelligent and extremely well trained or they wouldn't be there in the first place. When women come aboard a submarine there was only a small discretion needed in language and behavior to be acceptable to the fairer sex. This is all the more true of modern nuclear submarines. Each man in these submarines is a technician and expert in his own right. He demands and gets respect from officers and other enlisted men. Profanity is less needed because technical innovations have reduced the amount of work frustrations.

Courtesy is not abandoned just because men go under the water. On the contrary, going under the water demands a level of courtesy not found elsewhere.

CHAPTER 17
TWO NON-MEAT ENTRÉES

The Navy has long recognized that protein comes from several products in addition to meat. Beans have been a Navy staple since the Civil War and possibly before. Beans may be served as the main course for noon and evening meals and are sometimes found on submarine menus for breakfast. Beans were most often served in a sweet tomato base with ham or bacon as seasoning, however, pinto beans, lima beans, kidney beans and white beans were combined into stews. Black eyed peas, which are really beans, are popular protein sources on the boats.

Corn was a staple that was most often carried in cans. It could be made into creamed corn, corn soup, corn fritters and corn O'Brien. Hominy was a cured corn and was served as grits.

Potatoes were another staple. They had a long shelf life and could be carried without refrigeration for many weeks. They were bulky, but were often stored in spaces that would not accommodate cardboard crates. Since they came in burlap bags they could be pushed and molded into spaces around equipment.

In fleet type and Guppy boats the freeze lockers were reserved for meat. This meant that most all vegetables came in cans. These were in cardboard crates that lined showers, bilges, and passageways anywhere that didn't represent a hazard to the operation of the boat. The most popular vegetables (and those that best suited canning) were carrots, corn, beans, peas, broccoli, cabbage, tomatoes, and mixed vegetables. Those that were seldom taken aboard included beets, cauliflower, turnips, kale, okra, and spinach.

Rice was not as popular as potatoes. However, it had the feature of being easily stored and provided carbohydrate bulk at a savings in storage space. Rice was never a big hit in submarines because it just wasn't as American as steak and potatoes.

With improved frozen and refrigerated spaces in nuclear submarines restrictions on the types of vegetables carried have been lifted and modern submarine menus show a much greater variety of fresh and frozen vegetables.

WILLIAM BENTLEY'S NAVY BAKED BEANS (Q-8)

William Bentley served aboard the submarine tender Proteus (AS-19) in 1946. He was a pharmacist's mate, but always loved cooking. Here is his recipe for traditional Navy Baked Beans. The recipe serves from four to six people.

Ingredients	Measure/Weight	Method
Beans, white	1 and 1/2 cup	Pick through the beans to remove any foreign matter. Rinse beans under running water. Transfer beans to pot, add water to cover them and let stand overnight. On day of serving drain off the water and place in cooking pot.
Water	5 cups	
Ham, diced	1 cup	
Onion, diced	2 cups	
Garlic	1 tbsp	
Molasses	1/2 cup	
Sugar, brown	1/2 cup	
Tomato sauce	2 and 1/2 cups	
Mustard, dry	1 tsp	
Celery salt	1 tsp	
Bay leaves	2	
Vinegar	2 tbsp	
Salt	pinch	
Pepper	pinch	Place ingredients in pot with beans. Stir beans and ingredients thoroughly.
Bacon	3 strips	Lay bacon strips across the beans and ingredients. Bake the contents at 350 deg F for about 45 minutes to one hour. Make sure the bacon is completely cooked. Mix the cooked bacon into the beans. Return to oven and bake for another hour. If necessary add water to keep a heavy consistency and stir contents every fifteen minutes. Remove pot from oven and let stand for 15 minutes before serving.

Serve in bowls with corn bread.

FRANK DOSTAL'S CORN FRITTERS (Q-22)

Frank Dostal served as cook aboard several submarines both diesel and nuclear powered. They included the Diodon (SS-349), Argonaut (SS-475), Wahoo (SS-565), and Halibut (SSN-587). These days anything made in a deep fat fryer is regarded with suspicion because of our fear of bad cholesterol. In the fifties and sixties that fear was minimal and submariners loved corn fritters. Rooster Cogburn of the famous movie called them Corn Dodgers and always kept a bag full while stalking the bad guys. They could be eaten hot or cold and it was not unusual for a submariner to stuff one in his pocket for munching while on watch.

Ingredients	Measure/Weight	Method
Flour, wheat	1 cup	Sift flour and dry ingredients.
Salt	1/2 tsp	
Baking powder	1 tbsp	
Sugar	1 and 1/2 tbsp	
Eggs, whole, beaten	2	Mix eggs, milk, shortening and corn. Add flour to mixture. Mix approximately 30 seconds or only until no flour is visible. (Batter will not be smooth.)
Milk, whole	1/2 cup	
Shortening, melted	1 tbsp	
Corn, cream style	3/4 cup	
		Dip mixture in 2 tbsp scoops and drop into deep fat fryer at 370 deg. F for about 2 minutes on each side. Fritters should be crisp.

The above recipe should make about eight portions. The average submariner ate about five of the fritters at a sitting, but the average retired submariner eats about two. It is important to have the oil temperature high so that the fritters can remain as oil-free as possible.

CHAPTER 18
THE CREW'S FAVORITE FOODS

The crew made its opinion known to the ship's cook in strong terms. Sailors in fleet type submarines and Guppies were silent about the food they ate only when it was good and there was plenty of it. When the quality of what they ate fell below that undefined line of acceptability the men were not adverse to letting the cook know exactly what they wanted. Some cooks reported to SRC that many submariners seemed to regard cooks as beings without feelings.

Officers never criticized a meal. It was an unwritten law in submarines that any officer who spoke negatively about a meal and did so within earshot of the executive officer or captain would be handed the job of commissary officer. Since this was the lowest job in the submarine officer kingdom, negative comments were kept in check.

On the other hand, as strange as it may seem, submariners often told the cook when the food was good. This quality in the men was apparently learned over many years under the sea. Compliments most often flowed from the older men, from chiefs and first class petty officers. It was not uncommon for officers to walk from the forward battery to the galley and compliment the cook on a meal that had been well prepared. Although the commissary officer had very little to do with the actual production of meals he too received compliments from officers when a meal deserved comment.

The quality of food on a submarine was often out of the cook's hands, because he was largely constrained by the Navy supply system. Fortunately, the Navy had the foresight to provide submarines with enough money to buy quality foods from commercial vendors. Submarine cooks often bought directly from civilian food vendors. This increased the variety of foods available by a wide margin.

The foods that tended to be bought from vendors when the submarine was in port included,

       Baked goods such as bread, doughnuts and pastries.
       Ice cream in flavor varieties
       Fresh sea food and lobster
       Salad dressings
       Pies
       Assorted cereal
       Assorted specialty cakes such as Twinkies and cup cakes

When in ports where a particular food was abundant the cook could trade in common commodity such as coffee for the food. In Maine, for example, 20 pound coffee containers could be bartered for lobsters. In foreign ports the practice was available, but more difficult because of the lack of opportunity to develop a working relationship with the locals. In Japan the practice of cumshaw was honed to a fine edge by the submarine cooks who were able to get fresh seafoods for coffee.

Manipulation of the commissary budget by both the lead cook and the commissary officer allowed a submarine to serve extravagant meals from time to time. It was not uncommon for a truck to unload crates of live Maine lobsters on the pier next to the tender. Requests for working party volunteers to carry such goodies aboard were responded to with enthusiasm.

On the other hand, the freedom to buy from vendors could sometimes be abused by cooks. In order to appreciate the difficulty of food acquisition it must be perceived that the heavy goods had to be carried up a steep stairway into the tender, then through the tender to the opposite side, across one or more gangways to the submarine, then down the after battery hatch to the crew's mess where it then had to be stored in cool and freeze lockers or any space in the submarine that was not otherwise filled.

In spite of the difficulties described above the quality of the food eaten and the food delivered to the boat was quite good. As one would expect crew members most often appreciated the higher cost meals, but it is surprising that among the sailors' favorites were many meals that represented the cook's imagination rather than shear cost. The following breakfasts were the favorites of the crew.

> Eggs to order
> Creamed eggs
> Minced beef on toast (served in a variety of forms)
> Chipped beef on toast (also served in a variety of ways)

Naturally, most breakfasts featured fresh fruit, cereal, and a meat such as bacon or sausage. Some eggs to order meals were served with a small steak. Another favorite of breakfasts were the rolls, buns and coffee cakes that were often set out for the crew before breakfast was served.

The following favorite entrees for noon and evening meals are listed in order of preference from the SRC study of food service over fifty years.

> Steak, Filet
> Braised Beef
> Roast Beef
> Lobster
> Fried Chicken
> Roast Chicken
> Baked Ham
> Beef Stew
> Spaghetti with tomato sauce
> Pork Chops
> Chili Con Carne
> Pizza
> Meat Loaf

Barbecued Chicken
Pot Roast
Sea Food Dinner

The above was normally served with vegetables, potatoes, bread, fresh salad and dessert. The vegetables least likely to be served were artichokes, asparagus and collards. Seldom served vegetables included spinach, cauliflower, beats, Brussels sprouts, broccoli and celery. Often served vegetables included beans, corn, carrots, peas, potatoes and rice.

Foreign and regional meals were made to enliven the normal routine. The most popular were the Italian, Mexican, and Chinese dishes.

The study showed pies to be the favorite dessert with ice cream coming in a close second. Baked apples, puddings and cobblers were also at the top of favorites.

Soups were often served both in conjunction with a meal or separately in the afternoon and during the late evening hours. The favorite soups were heavy bean soups and vegetable soups. Salads served during meals were normally lettuce, tomato, and onion with a choice of dressings. Occasionally a salad on weekends would be special such as deviled eggs, chicken salad or tuna salad.

It should be noted that desires change over the years and often are different by virtue of geography. The men like one thing in port and another at sea. One predominant preference was the desire for anything fresh when the submarine first entered port after a long patrol.

The commissary department of submarines knocked themselves out while on difficult patrols to make the men happy. Some examples of out-of-the-ordinary goodies served were:

Baked Alaska
Popcorn during movies
Doughnuts and hot chocolate at midnight
Upside down cake
Hand made ice cream
Cherry pie
Cherry jubilee
Cherry cobbler with whipped cream
Mom's sweet potato and pumpkin pie
Cream puffs
Fudge

On the Benjamin Franklin (SSBN-640) the cook served "Doc's Low-cal Pie." This was a baked graham cracker crust filled with soft ice cream, then frozen, covered with cherry pie filling, whipped cream and chopped nuts. Nothing was too good for the boys of the Franklin.

The in-port Sunday afternoon meal was normally something special. It was a time for the duty cook to prepare difficult entrees. The duty section was only one third of the crew and the galley was only needed to prepare two meals. Thus, the Sunday afternoon meal could be somewhat different than the ordinary. Not only did the men like Steak and Lobster on these days they appreciated,

    Grilled chicken with steak and sausage
    Roast turkey
    Fried chicken
    Roast chicken
    Trout
    Roast beef
    Candied ham

Often the Sunday meal could be simple as it might be at home with just sandwiches and potato salad or grilled cheese sandwiches or hamburgers. Sometimes the boat had a barbecue with the grill topside and tables set up to eat in the sun. Some boats opened the galley to the men who made themselves simple meals. On some nuclear boats a department assumed responsibility for a meal. Thus, the torpedomen might bust a gut in the galley to out-do the communicators. Real cooks were never too far away if the men got into trouble and the practice was restricted to uneventful patrols.

Of course the Sunday brunch was informal with eggs to order and the trimmings. Generally speaking, the boat tried to bring a little of home onto the submarine during these leisurely hours.

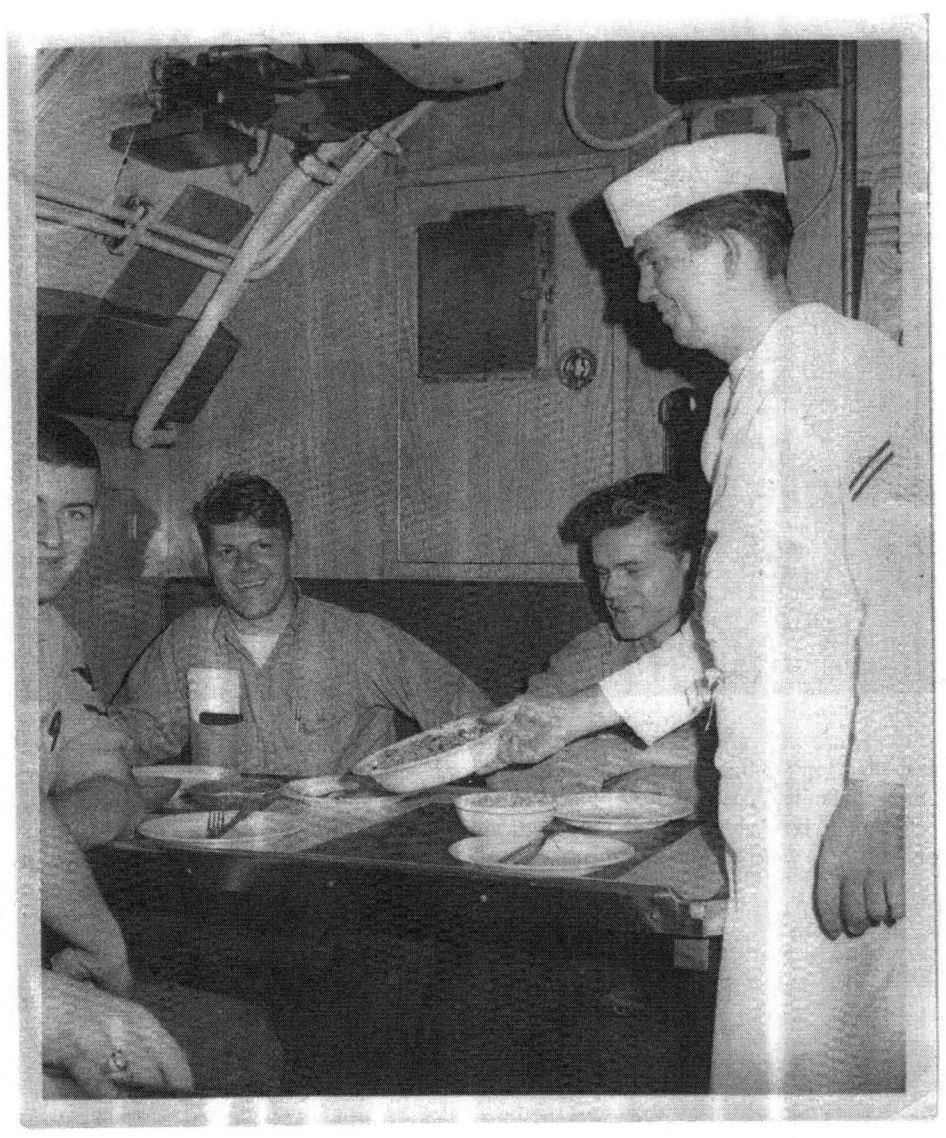

Ronald Reiner, FA and duty mess cook put on his whites and hat for this photo-op in the crew's mess of the Salmon (SS-573) during the 1960s. Seated are from left to right, David Richardson, IC3, Art Solomon IC3 and Gary Azbill, EM3. Ron Reiner is serving a bowl of cole slaw as a noon meal starter. Note the after battery compartment bill holder on bulkhead.

The forward, starboard side of a Guppy's crew's mess. From left to right the major equipment are: table and bench of crew's mess, the crew's coffee urn, the water tight door leading to control, the deck hatch leading to the cool and freeze lockers, fuel ballast tank 3A fuel filling and transfer valve, test cocks for the tank, the emergency hand operated flood valve which is padlocked by the auxiliarymen, the 600 pound air blow stop valve to the tank and the scullery with its counter top.

Phil Beals, CM3 stirs his soup for an afternoon soup-down on USS Bang (SS-385) during the 1950's.

Bill Dickerson, TM1 takes time out from the noon meal to smile for the camera. Men in the background serve themselves from platters of food. The submarine is not identified. Those with sharp eyes may want to email SRC with the name of the boat.

The galley of the Wahoo (SS-565) suffered from sea water and condensation dripping from the overhead. Wally Bishop, CS3 dressed in rain gear makes French toast for breakfast for the crew while on patrol.

Men of the USS Charr (SS-328) celebrate their 7000th dive. The forward port side of the crew's mess shows the built-in checker board on the Formica table in forground. Standing in rear are Lcdr. James Callan. On his left are seated, Vince Solari, Jake Wade, Ellis "Doc" Taft, Harley Rackley and Dan McClain. In forground, right is Lin Marvil.

USS Chivo (SS-341) Dependents' Day Cruise during the 1950s. Looking aft on the port side of the crew's mess. Lynn Lockwood and George "Bart" Lockwood are on the right. Note the juke box which for a nickel gave five plays. On the table is hot coffee in the urn, milk in half-pint containers and commercial salad dressing.

Commander Submarines Pacific, Admiral Grenfell digs into a cake commemorating the USS Wahoo (SS-565)'s 1956 WesPac cruise. Seated from left to right are Ted Dick, Joe Birkle and John Smailer.

CHAPTER 19
OFF BEAT SALADS THAT CREWS LIKED

For the most part, salads in submarines were extremely simple. They consisted of head lettuce, tomatoes and unions; coarsely chopped and heaved into large stainless steel bowls. A bit of oil and a ton of vinegar were added or when in port, individual bottles of commercially prepared dressings were put on every table.

Special salads were sometimes prepared and this was often done to offset a dreary entree. If grilled cheese sandwiches or hot dogs were to be the main course of a noon meal the cooks would make sure that a special salad was prepared to accompany the sandwiches. There were a large number of special salads to be found in the Standard Navy Recipe Service. Among them were hot green bean, ham, macaroni, pineapple and cheese, chicken, potato, shrimp and tuna.

While it was possible for the submarine cook to prepare salad dressings from scratch it was seldom done. For one thing commercial dressings were preferred by the men, and for another a lousy dressing could ruin an otherwise good salad. Besides, if a crew member selected a commercial dressing from several on the table he was responsible for the outcome.

The SRC survey found that submariners had preferences in salads. They liked salads with chicken hunks, salads with blended cottage cheese and vegetables, a reasonably dry cole slaw and macaroni. Potato salad was also a favorite. In addition they liked salad accompaniments. The most favored were deviled eggs which could be served with a green salad or as an appetizer for the entree.

The macaroni salad wasn't really a salad at all. It might have a few canned vegetables, but the main ingredient was macaroni and mayonnaise. Be that as it may, the men in the after battery ate lots of macaroni salad, and in the latter days of a patrol it served as a salad when most everything fresh had been consumed.

Six recipes are offered and each was a favorite of submariners: a chicken salad, deviled eggs, a cottage cheese and vegetable salad, cole slaw, a macaroni salad and potato salad.

Salads were most susceptible to invasion of diesel and cork fumes. The recipes suggested here are absent of such flavor and therefore may not ring 100% true with diesel boat veterans.

JIM TIERNEY'S MACARONI SALAD

Jim qualified on the Odax (SS-484) during the late forties. He was a yeoman aboard Sea Cat (SS-399), and made chief when serving on ComSubRon Twelve staff. He was one of the fortunate few who had the duty of typing the weekly menu using a manual machine with many carbon copies. An example of such a menu is to be seen in the illustration section. He remembers the crew's remorseless chiding of the cook's attempts at savory chicken soup. Over the 1MC would come the word, "Would the duty chicken please report to the galley and run through today's soup?"

Here is Jim's Macaroni Salad taken from a Standard Navy Recipe.

Ingredients	Measure/Weight	Method
Macaroni	1 and 1/4 cups	
Water	Enough to cover	
Salt	1/4 tsp	Add 2 tbsp salad oil to boiling water to prevent macaroni from sticking. Add salt to water and stir before adding macaroni.
Onions, finely chopped	1/4 cup	
Pepper	1 tbsp	
Pimento, chopped	1/8 cup	
Celery salt	1/2 tsp	
Eggs, hard boiled finely chopped	1/2 cup	
Pickles, finely chopped	1/2 cup	
Cheese, shredded	3/4 cup	
Mayonnaise	2 tbsp	Thoroughly mix ingredients in large bowl. Add the cooked macaroni and blend together. Serve over lettuce leaves.

For a rougher texture substitute finely chopped celery for the celery salt. For a sweeter taste use butter pickles and for a sharper taste use dill pickles.

JIM TIERNEY'S COLE SLAW

Cole slaw is a trick to make. The correct proportion of cabbage to dressing is essential to prevent swamping. Good Cole Slaw requires the dressing to be sufficiently viscous to cling to the cabbage. The other concern is the relation of sugar to vinegar. The amount of sugar must bring the dressing only to the brink of sweetness. This recipe should work well; however, a little experimentation will refine it to the individual's taste.

Ingredients	Measure/Weight	Method
Cabbage	3/4 lb or a half head	Grate cabbage to coarse shreds.
Onions, finely chopped	3 Tsp	
Peppers, green finely chopped	3/4 cup	
Vinegar	1/8 cup	Use half white vinegar and half rice vinegar
Salad oil	1/8 cup	
Sugar	1 and 1/2 tsp	Substitute 6 packets of sugar substitute, if desired.
Salt	1/4 tsp	
Pepper	1/8 tsp	
Catsup	3 tsp	This may be eliminated to taste.
Raisins	1/8 cup	Allow time for raisins to absorb liquids and become plump. Mix raisins with vinegar, salad oil, salt, pepper and celery seed.
Celery seed	1 tsp	
		Mix blended ingredients with coarsely shredded cabbage. Allow to stand for five minutes before serving.

It is a good idea to chill the mixed salad before serving. Typical serving size is small since the cabbage is filling. Excess dressing may be refrigerated and used later.

JOE BIRKLE'S COTTAGE CHEESE SALAD (M-41)

Joe Birkle qualified on the Sea Poacher (SS-406) and was a torpedoman on several boats including the Wahoo (SS-565). He was kind enough to try his skill at following a Standard Navy Recipe. He notes that submarine cooks avoided serving this on the first night in port after a patrol. The blazing color of the salad would have been too much for the hung-over sailors. Here is his cottage cheese salad geared to family size.

Ingredients	Measure/Weight	Method
Cucumbers, diced	1 small	
Radishes, chopped	6 medium	
Onions, scallion, chopped	1 bunch	
Celery, diced	2 inner stalks	
Peppers, green finely chopped	2 tbsp	
Peppers, yellow, finely chopped	2 tbsp	Mix vegetables in large bowl.
Cottage cheese	16 ounces	
Cantaloupe	1 medium	
Salt	pinch	
Pepper	pinch	
Mayonnaise	1 tbsp	Mix vegetables with cottage cheese, salt, pepper and mayonnaise. Cut melon in half and clean. Spoon vegetable and cheese mixture into melon halves. Serve chilled.

If melon is not available the mixture may be served on lettuce leaves. It may also be served with peach or pear halves.

KEN LEE'S CHICKEN SALAD (M-39)
From Submarine Supplement Recipe, USS Toro (SS-422)

Captain Lee commanded the USS Gato (SSN-615) during the early eighties. He served as an officer on many submarines before that, both diesel and nuclear powered. This great recipe was tested by him on real submariners. In his own words,

"I attended the Saturday meeting of South Florida Base of U.S. Sub Vets inc. I brought along my Chicken Salad and my brief history of the USS Toro which I grabbed off the internet. The subvets enjoyed the history notes and ate every bit of the Chicken Salad - definitely two thumbs up from the submarine veterans. The oldest Sub Vet at this meeting was FT2(SS) Bob McNeil from Segundo (SS-398). Bob made all 5 war patrols, during which he and his shipmates sunk 17 Japanese ships. When my Chicken Salad got Bob's approval my day was made!"

The following recipe serves about eight people:

Ingredients	Measure/Weight	Method
Peppers, green	1/4 cup	Chop peppers and set aside.
Peppers, red	1/4 cup	
Chicken, boned (either canned or fresh cooked)	3 cups or 2 lbs.	Remove chicken hunks from can or remove chicken parts from boiled chicken. Dice the chicken into inch cubes and combine with peppers.
Vinegar	1 tbsp	Mix into chicken and peppers and allow to marinate for one hour.
Pickles, sweet	1/4 cup	
Eggs, hard boiled, chopped	4 large	
Salt	1 tsp	
Salad dressing	1 cup	Combine all of the vegetables, salad dressing and seasoning, mixing well. Add to chicken and peppers, continuing to mix. Refrigerate for ten minutes and serve.
Pepper	4 tsp	
Peas, drained	1/2 cup	
Pimiento, finely diced	1/4 cup	
Celery salt	2 tsp	
Carrots, drained	1/2 cup	
Paprika	2 tsp	

PHIL GRIFFITH'S DEVILED EGGS
(F-10)

The following recipe is from the 1963 Standard Navy Recipe Service. Deviled eggs were an accompaniment to several meals and were served on trays. Occasionally, they took the place of salads. Because it took a great deal of time to prepare, the crew considered deviled eggs to be a delicacy. Submarine cooks were amazed at how many half-eggs each crew member could toss down. Phil served aboard several diesel and nuclear powered submarines.

The following recipe is geared for one dozen eggs.

Ingredients	Measure/Weight	Method
Eggs, medium	12 eggs	Hard boil the eggs. Peel and cut eggs in half lengthwise. Remove and mash yokes.
Mayonnaise	1/2 cup	Add the remaining ingredients, except the garnish, to the mashed yokes. Beat until fluffy.
Worcestershire sauce	1 tsp	
Lemon juice	1 tsp	
Mustard, dry	1/2 tsp	
Onion, finely minced	1/8 cup	
Pimento, finely chopped	1/3 ounce	
		Refill the egg whites with the deviled mixture allowing approximately 1 and 1/2 tbsp for each half egg.
Salt	dash	
Parsley or Paprika	dash	Garnish each egg half

Phil added:
"We prepared an equivalent recipe using as a guide a similar one from the Southern Living, '1982 Annual Recipes Book'. This made it easier to scale the project down to a dozen eggs."

POTATO SALAD (M-26)

No list of submarine recipes would be complete without reference to potato salad. The Standard Navy Recipe Service covered both hot and cold varieties. It also had levels of complexity – the basic rendition and the deluxe salad. Although the following recipe is for the basic recipe it has been modified to more closely fit the description of a deluxe potato salad.

Ingredients	Measure/Weights	Method
Potatoes, cooked, cold	1 pound	Peel and dice potatoes into 1/2 inch cubes
Bacon, chopped	¼ cup	Cook bacon until crisp
Shallot or onion	½ medium sized	
Pickles, sweet	2 medium	
Mayonnaise	4 tbsp	
Salt	pinch	
Pepper	pinch	
Mustard	2 tsp	Thoroughly mix bacon bits, onion, Mayonnaise, salt, pepper and mustard.
Celery, finely chopped	one stalk	
Pimiento, finely chopped	1 tbsp	Toss potatoes, celery and pimiento into the dressing being care to not bruise the potatoes. Allow to stand for one hour before serving.

This recipe is the standard for making great potato salad. The amount of Mayonnaise will determine the viscosity and the tendency of "store-bought" potato salad is to be too soupy. Submariners prefer a somewhat dry salad. To increase the crunchiness of the salad use two stalks of celery and to give the salad a small bite add a half tsp of white vinegar.

CHAPTER 20
SPECIAL DISHES AND SPECIAL MEALS

Every American submarine capitalized on the diversity of the American people as reflected in the crew. The United States was geographically diverse and the regional foods of our country have been an attraction not only to those who were familiar with the special item, but with others who wish to experience the taste of a new dish.

Submarines based in Norfolk, Charleston, Kings Bay and Key West were likely to have had menus emphasizing dishes peculiar to the South. Black eyed peas and grits replaced other cereals in those boats operating out of ports south of the Mason-Dixon line. You could even find collard greens served alongside channel catfish on a few boats.

Hamburgers and hot dogs were probably considered by most to be at the very heart of the American diet. These were to be found on submarine menus, however, not in the abundance that one might imagine. Southwest chili and tacos had about as much hot sauce as a person was likely to find in a submarine meal. It was not wise to be too experimental in the use of hot spices. The boats had only a few heads to serve the entire crew. Middle of the road dishes such as Kentucky fried chicken were good, steady choices. At the opposite end of the spice options was the New England boiled dinner. Here you could find boiled corned beef, boiled cabbage, boiled potatoes and a boiled vegetable such as carrots. This had to have been the blandest meal ever served on a submarine and only the most dedicated Bostonians relished it.

Of course the menu was really a product of the captain's likes and dislikes, so if he's from a cotton plantation the crew was likely to get used to fried ochre and steamed shrimp.

Many so-called foreign dishes have become so much a part of the American culture that they can hardly be regarded as special. Tacos, burritos, pizza, spaghetti, lasagne and chili are all to be found in the modern submarine's menu. Since the modern nuclear powered submarines often serve more than one entree the second choice is often one of Italian, Mexican or Oriental style.

Some of the more off-beat meals served aboard submarines were Sauerbraten, Irish corned beef, Chop Suey, and Beef Stroganoff, (One boat had a recipe from a White Russian living in Tsingtao, China). The submarine cook took great pride in this and the crew appreciated the authenticity.) Chow Mien, Sweet and Sour Pork, and Filipino Adobo. The favorites of the crew were the Italian dishes, the Chinese including fried rice, stir fried shrimp and sweet-sour pork. Occasionally, boats served real Mexican meals such as chicken tortillas and refried beans.

Not all cooks were at home with regional and foreign dishes. For example the trick in making Chinese dishes is to get the thickening agent into the sauce so that it became not only more viscous, but smooth as well. Arrow-root can be used, but most cooks preferred good old fashioned corn starch. When the cook fell short of perfection in these special meals it was better not to try them at all. In the book, "Of Wives and Submarines" the cook, Greenwood makes the life of the commissary officer, Ltjg. Gilhooly miserable by his inability to prepare chow mien.

"The noon meal had been called and already eager officers were sliding into their wardroom seats, not knowing that what awaited them was Greenwood's Chinese special.

"Gilhooly took the remaining empty chair. Some of the officers were on the Sperry conducting business and one of the absentees was the executive officer. The captain inquired of his officers how the ship's work was commencing, and they responded in pleasant tones, how each of their departments was up to snuff. When it came to Gil's turn he couldn't think of anything very interesting to say and so recited today's lunch menu. He told of the apple pie a la mode and the tossed salad, leaving the entree for last. When he mentioned the words "chicken chow mien", groans came from the officers.

"The captain sat in stoic silence as a pall of gloom settled over the wardroom. Officers became intent on stirring their coffee, and it was a while before the conversation returned to normal. The steward served the salads and each man shook his favorite dressing bottle. Pouring the different dressings with a special care, the officers anticipated that the salads might be the only food preceding the dessert. Gilhooly, never having eaten Greenwood's chicken chow mien, looked forward to the main dish.

"When it came, the steward served it with great resolve. He wedged himself into the slim space behind the officers' chairs and scooped the viscous fluid over noodles in each man's plate. It smelled delicious and the vegetables had an attractive, corn-starch shine. The liquid was ladled onto Gil's plate, and he again enjoyed the aromatic steam as it lifted itself to his nostrils. Gill went right to work on the mixture, but the other officers stared ambivalently at their rations and their spoons. Finally, in resignation, the ship's engineer dipped his fork into the food.

"The captain had the poise of George Washington as he summoned the chow mien to his lips. The first taste was the toughest; after that, the mouth resigned itself to the texture. Following his example, each officer in his own way, assumed the duty of eating at least a portion of the meal.

"Gilhooly, the commissary officer, and therefore the originator of this meal, moved the hot vegetables around in his mouth so that he might get hold of a chicken morsel. As he did so his tongue kept slipping over lumps of semi-solid matter. At first he thought it must be over-sized tapioca, but the solid masses were tasteless. He looked about to see if others might be experiencing something akin to his questioning taste buds, and discovered that all eyes were upon him. Even the captain, who had regained a measure of sensitivity, was appealing to Gilhooly's mercy.

"'Good, isn't it?' uttered Gilhooly, meekly.

"Fred said, 'This is the lumpiest, most foul excuse for oriental food ever to find its way into this wardroom.' There was a pause during which no one spoke. Now all eyes shifted to Fred. Then he added, 'But . . . good.'"

As has been stated in another section of this publication, negative comments about the food from officers gain the commenting officer the commissary department. And no officer in his right mind wanted to be commissary officer, thus the appendix, 'But good'.

CHAPTER 21
TIME-THE COOK'S MASTER

The submarine cook, like all other cooks in both the military and civilian life lived under a constant clock. Since the human body is a clock of sorts it demands fuel on a regular basis. The submarine, being a machine not unlike the human body has time-related demands of its own. Food preparation was largely based on a combination of heat and time. Finally, the actual consumption of food took a finite amount of time.

All of this made the submarine cook a clock watcher. He was constantly fighting the clock, trying to stay on time, trying to fit his meal preparation and service into the routine of the submarine. There was a certain stress to keeping up with a schedule and the submarine cook was never out from under it.

Submarines, like other ships were manned by a crew that was divided into sections or watches. Since there were two twelve hour periods in each day the crew was divided into thirds. In normal steaming conditions two thirds of the crew was either asleep or tending to the maintenance needs of the ship. One third of the crew at any given time was operating the ship.

This routine was interrupted by circumstances that demand the ship's operation by the best and most experienced of the crew. These circumstances included getting under way, entering port and manning battle stations. The operating watch for getting under way and entering port was called the maneuvering watch and involved more of the crew than just one third. The battle station bill was fragmented into special types of operations and involved every crew member, so the essential relation between battle stations and food service was that food service stopped when battle stations began. True, there were shades of food service when the combat continued for a prolonged period, but in such circumstances the menu was ignored and sandwiches were served at the battle station.

The normal operating routine was called the regular sea detail. The on-coming watch was the relieving watch and the off-going watch was the fill in.

The design of a submarine crew's mess takes this organization into account so that the number of crew members that could be served at any given time was about one third that of the crew. It didn't work out in quite such a tidy manner, but that was the basic intent. The first section to be served was the relieving section. This group of men had to eat between the time that the meal was finally prepared and fifteen minutes before the hour of the watch relief. The men ate on a schedule. They downed their food and left the mess so that the mess cooks could set up for the next section. Parenthetically, the men lined up aft of the crew's mess down the passageway. In a Fleet Type boat and Guppy this meant standing and gabbing in the crew's berthing portion of the after battery compartment while waiting for the go sign from the lead cook.

In an FBM submarine the men line up aft in the mid-ship's passageway. Lines are actual serving lines, cafeteria style. The difference being that in an FBM submarine most food is served in buffet. Men select their food items from chill and steam trays with mess cooks behind the breeze-way serving the entrée. Nuclear fast attack submarines are organized using a combination of the two types of food service.

Since this study centers on food service in non-nuclear submarines the time commitments described are relevant to the type of service where men are served food in serving dishes by mess cooks.

When the relieving section of men had been fed the next section was the one third of the crew not on watch and not going on watch. This was simply referred to as the second section. They had a more leisurely structured time to eat, however, they could not ignore the hunger of those who were just being relieved of the watch. This last third of the crew was made up of tired and hungry men eager to relax in the crew's mess and eat a good meal. The second section was pushed along gently by the lead cook until all had left the crew's mess at which time the mess cooks quickly set up for the off-going watch section.

After about half of the relieved section had eaten and evacuated the crew's mess those members of the crew who had not been able to eat on the regular schedule for whatever reason were free to fill in the eating spaces vacated by the relieved section.

It was normally a mess cook who announced the serving of a meal over the 1MC. The exact words varied from boat to boat and the mess cooks, who were youngsters, took pride in their moments at the mike. Some announcements were erudite, such as "Now, the noon meal is being served in the crew's dinette," while others were more matter-of-fact such as, "First call for the relieving section." Some boats never used the 1MC to announce meals, but to most submariners the words were pleasant forecasts of impending delicacies.

The question arises as to how much time it took for a submariner to eat his meal. In our survey described in the introduction, SRC found that in non-nuclear submarines while underway the mean breakfast eating time was thirty six minutes with a rather narrow distribution from boat to boat of from twenty two minutes to forty minutes. In rough terms, it took the ordinary submariner about a half hour to eat his breakfast. This means that the cooks and mess cooks were serving breakfast to the three sections and fill-ins over about a two hour period.

The Fleet Type and Guppy underway noon meal took a little longer to consume. The mean (average) eating time was thirty six minutes with a variation of from twenty nine minutes to forty three minutes. The total time that the crew's mess was actually serving food during the noon meal was about two and a half hours.

The evening meal on an underway Fleet Type or Guppy submarine was consumed in about forty one minutes. The distribution from boat to boat is large, (from thirty minutes to over an hour) because this meal tended to be the most social meal served on the submarine. Even when the boat remained submerged for prolonged periods the social action at the end of the meal kept the crew's mess open.

The daily routine of an operating submarine might have included a movie. If this was the case the movie was shown in the crew's mess and this was normally scheduled for eight PM. In order for the movie to be shown, the crew's mess and galley were cleaned. This placed a limit on relaxation for the last section to be served.

The use of the galley and crew's mess when underway was constant. Using twenty four hour time one can visualize the galley's use from the following:

Nightly baking -	2230 to 0430
Breakfast prep and set up -	0500 to 0600
Breakfast serving -	0600 to 0800
Breakfast clean up -	0800 to 0900
Noon meal prep and set up -	1030 -1130
Noon meal serving -	1115 - 1400
Noon meal clean up -	1400 - 1500
Evening meal prep and set up -	1530 - 1730
Evening meal serving -	1730 - 1945
Evening meal clean up -	1945 - 2100

The galley range, ovens and fryers hardly had time to cool before the next preparation began.

The crew's mess was slightly less used for meal purposes and time periods were available for training. A meeting might take place amidst the clatter of the galley being cleaned and the scullery in full use. The scullery in a Fleet type and Guppy submarine was on the starboard side of the passageway. This meant that the final stages of clean up could be restricted to this area and the tables could be used for training and recreation. Food preparation normally occupied the galley while the crew's mess would not be controlled by the mess cooks until about one hour before meal time. The crew's mess was open for the crew's recreational use normally during the following hours:

0900 to 1030
1500 to 1630
2045 to 0500

The crew's mess was used for showing movies, holding tournaments, training/lectures and Sunday worship services. Most of the time the crew's mess non-operational hours meant that men could draw a cup of coffee and relax at one of the tables. Rest was a difficult commodity to come by and crew members took advantage of times when the crew's mess was out of action.

The in-port routine was much more leisurely. The morning meal service was for those in the duty section and those that had come aboard early enough to have breakfast before colors. Generally speaking, breakfast began at six and ended at seven fifty five, five minutes before colors.

When scheduled to get underway the submarine's crew had reported aboard during the night and early morning hours. Breakfast started and ended according to the in-port routine except that immediately following colors and morning muster, topside aft of the sail, the maneuvering watch was set and the boat got underway. The cooks and mess cooks lay below, finished the breakfast clean up and started preparing the noon meal. Some boats allowed cooks and mess cooks to remain below during muster in order that the work could remain on schedule.

While in-port the noon meal and evening meal were served from about eleven hundred to thirteen hundred hours and sixteen hundred to eighteen hundred hours respectively. The noon meal was typically served to the entire crew, but because liberty commenced at sixteen hundred few men remained for the evening meal.

On weekends while in port the submarine was relaxed and meals were much less formal. The Sunday schedule was altered to only two meals, a brunch served from about ten hundred to noon and an evening meal served in the late afternoon. Since the afternoon Sunday meal had only the duty section and those who stayed aboard for personal reasons it was likely to be special. This was a time when lobster or equivalent expensive meal was often served. On the other hand the menu may have reflected those items not high on the captain's favorites list.

Holiday meal service while in port required a special menu with the entrée in keeping with the season and all the trimmings. Guests were invited and this placed a special time burden on the cooks.

Serving and eating time was critical to the job of submarine cook because preparation time and clean-up time were both extensions of eating time. Preparation time required forethought and planning. Meats to be thawed must have been taken from the freezer twelve hours before preparation. Preparation time for breakfast required the least time, however, baking started at about midnight for the following day. When underway the four to eight watch relieving section awakened to the delicious smells of fresh cinnamon-sticky buns and coffee.

When underway the galley was seldom cold. Baking, meal preparation and crew's mess clean-up kept the cooks and mess cooks going on a twenty four hour schedule. In order for baked goods and meals to have been served within ten minutes of production the lead cook and baker had to be real clock watchers.

CHAPTER 22
HEARTY SOUPS FOR IN-BETWEEN MEALS

The casual observer of submariner behavior would conclude that soup and submarines don't go together. A rolling and tossing diesel submarine on the surface would preclude the serving of soups and the picture of a rugged engineman sipping a delicate soup would be incongruous. But, as illogical as it might seem, soups were a favorite of submarine crew members during and after the Second World War.

Soup in submarines was a device of economics. It was intended to provide crew members with hot and invigorating nourishment while capitalizing on the left-overs from the previous day's meals. Crew members never groused about eating left-overs. Each man knew that the best soups came from yesterday's meals. They had learned that lesson from the Great Depression and many of the soups served on board a submarine were reminiscent of home.

Soups were the hallmark of a good cook. While the Standard Navy Recipe Service sported over twenty different soups the reality of a submarine meant that the cook added to the left-overs whatever vegetables and seasonings would be needed to make a hearty soup. This was his opportunity to show his initiative and some were more successful than others.

Submariners preferred a thick soup. They liked to pour it from a milk pitcher into a cup and then to jab a spoon in the middle of the liquid. When the spoon stood on its own the soup was prejudged to be good. For this reason many soups emphasized cooked beans that were crushed or beaten to give the soup a heavy viscosity. The men took the mug to their duty stations when possible and ate on the job.

Soup was served at odd hours. There was often a soup-down in the afternoon between meals and sometimes the cooks made a soup that was served at midnight. The aroma of a seasoned soup making its way through the submarine was a great boost to the mid-watch relieving section. When one heard over the 1MC the call for, "Soup down" he knew it was an invitation to a bit of good taste and relaxation.

Presented here are seven soups, all of which have beans in some form. They come to us from several veteran cooks. Some are really like a stew while others are less formidable. All are strictly submarine and reflect what the men really ate.

CASEY JOHNSTON'S BEAN SOUP WITH HAMBURGER (P-23) AND HAMBURGER SOUP

Casey served as cook on the Stickleback (SS-415), Sea Fox (SS-402) and qualified on the Sabalo (SS-302). He has had many years of cooking experience and has memorized most of the recipes used in submarines. He offers two related recipes that were high on the list of submariners' favorites. Each has the distinction of being in the Navy's tradition of nutritious and hearty soups and each was intended to make use of yesterday's uneaten hamburger. The first is a heavy mixed bean soup while the second is a hamburger soup, the aroma of which in the morning hours of a patrol would make men salivate.

Bean Soup with Hamburger

Ingredients	Measure/Weight	Method
Hamburger	1 pound	
Onion, large, diced	1	Brown hamburger and onion together in a frying pan.
Chilies, green, diced	4 ounces	
Kidney beans	16 ounces	Combine ingredients in large pot. Allow to stand. Add meat and onion combination. Add sufficient tomato juice. Allow mixture to simmer for several hours, adding water if necessary. Add spices to taste.
Navy beans	16 ounces	
White beans	16 ounces	
Tomatoes, crushed	16 ounces	
Tomato juice	1 quart	

CASEY JOHNSTON'S HAMBURGER SOUP

Ingredients	Measure/Weight	Method
Hamburger	1 pound	
Onion, large	1	Brown hamburger and onion in a skillet.
Corn	1-15 ounce can	
String beans	1-15 ounce can	
Peas	1-15 ounce can	
Tomatoes, crushed	1-15 ounce can	
Chicken stock	1-15 ounce can	Use liquid in cans. Add chicken stock as necessary. Simmer for one hour.
		Add spices to taste.
Sage	1 tsp	
Salt	1/2 tsp	
Pepper	1/2 tsp	

JOHN APPLEMAN'S BEEF STEW (J-19)

John Appleman served on the Jallao (SS-368) where he qualified during the 1950s. He was a submarine cook during his tenure on the boat and prepared a lot of beef stew. Here's his basic recipe as well as a few ideas for interesting variations.

Ingredients	Measure/Weight	Method
Beef, boneless, diced	1.5 pounds	Cut the beef into one inch cubes.
Flour, sifted	1/4 cup	Sprinkle flour over meat.
Salt	1/4 tsp	Shake salt and pepper on meat.
Pepper	1/4 tsp	
Vegetable oil	2 tbsp	Heat oil on medium heat.
Garlic, shaved	2 large cloves	Brown beef and add garlic.
Bouillon cubes, beef	2	Mix bouillon cubes with hot water.
Water, hot	1 cup	Add water and scrape bottom of pot. Allow mixture to cool for 5 to 10 min.
Tomatoes, canned	14 oz can	Mix ingredients. Add bay leaves and Worcestershire sauce.
Bay leaf	1 whole	
Worcestershire sauce	two dashes	Bring to boil. Simmer for 1 and 1/2 hours.
Onions, quartered	2 med.	
Carrots, sliced	3 med	
Celery, sliced	2 stalks	
Potatoes, diced	3 med.	Add vegetables, cover and simmer for 30 minutes longer or until vegetables are tender.

Substitute red wine for a portion of water according to taste, if desired. Add fresh herbs of choice. Sprinkle chopped fresh parsley before serving. For "peppier" stew add a dash of Tabasco sauce.

The stew recipe can be used for beef pie by reducing the amount of water/wine and using a tsp of cornstarch to thicken. Place stew into serving bowls and cover with pastry or biscuit dough as suggested by Sam Palmer.

JAMES MAYO'S BAKED BEAN SOUP (J-9)
AND SUBMARINE SOUP DOWN

Jim Mayo served on several submarines including the Tunny (SSG-282) on which he qualified, the Torsk (SS-423), the Sirago (SS-485) and the Barb (SSN-596). To quote his short bio:

"My career as a cook in the Navy, serving on four different submarines, was very interesting and gratifying. On long deployments on submarines the men needed something to break the monotony such as good food, special meals, and desired food items. After retiring from the Navy I continued a career in food service as a manager of two different universities and Morrison's Cafeteria. Cooking has continued to by my specialty and passion.

"The Navy recipe cards were revised and updated about every five or six years. I think the last revision was around 1959 or 60. Then, sometime in the sixties the Recipe Card Service became the Armed Forces Recipe Service. Just previously, in 1958 I attended school for three months at the Royal Hawaiian Hotel in Honolulu, working in the baking, cake decorating, catering, fry cooking, and buffet departments. Two recipes I created were published and put into the Navy Recipe Card Service; Hawaiian Spare Ribs and Teriyaki Steak.

"The Baked Bean Soup recipe was probably formulated to utilize the left over baked beans on the breakfast menu. Surface craft had beans and corn bread for Friday breakfasts because of field day. This became a tradition back in the Second World War. Baked beans and corn bread for breakfast was popular.

"This recipe is converted to four portions where I used measurements only. For the novice cook the measurement system is much easier. I made this soup recipe twice, the second time with improvements. It is a pretty good recipe although I don't remember using it. I usually made regular Navy Bean Soup or my own recipe for soup-downs, which is also included."

JAMES MAYO'S LEFT-OVER BAKED BEAN SOUP (P-9)

Ingredients	Measure/Weight	Method
Beans, previously baked	2 and 1/2 cups	Grind previously cooked beans adding enough water
Water	Enough to cover	to provide a rich soup base.
Stock, beef	2 and 1/4 cups	
Onions, chopped	2 and 1/2 tbsp	
Celery, chopped	2 and 1/2 tbsp	
Tomatoes, canned	1 cup	Chop tomatoes finely.
Tomato puree	4 ounces	
Salt	pinch	
Pepper	pinch	Add tomatoes, tomato puree, salt, pepper, celery and onions to stock. Heat to boiling.
Butter	1 and 1/2 tbsp	
Flour	1 tbsp	Combine butter and flour to make a roux. Add to soup. Cook, stirring occasionally, until soup is thickened.

This recipe is affected by the type of bean or combination of beans used, the thickness of the mixture, the amount of sugar, if used, and the addition of spices. It can be adjusted to suit the individual's taste.

JAMES MAYO'S SUBMARINE SOUP DOWN

According to Jim Mayo the beauty of this recipe is that it is simple and fast. He calls it the Navy Submarine Soup Down. When the submarine cook didn't have time to soak and pre-cook the dry beans he used regular canned pork and beans that come in size 10 cans.

Here is the simple recipe for four.

Ingredients	Measure/Weight	Method
Pork and beans canned	3 cups	Grind and mash 2 and 1/2 cup beans from the pork and beans mix. Set aside the remaining amount.
Bacon	3 slices	Fry bacon and set aside leaving the grease in the pan.
Onions, chopped	3 tbsp	
Celery, chopped fine	3 tbsp	
Carrots, chopped fine	3 tbsp	
Chicken stock	2 and 1/2 cups	Water may be substituted for chicken stock.
Tomato sauce	1/2 cup	
Salt	dash	
Pepper	dash	Sauté the onions, carrots, celery in the bacon fat until 1/2 cooked.
		Add all the remaining ingredients into the sauce pan and simmer slowly on low heat for 15 minutes.

The soup should have the correct consistency. It is a heavy and nicely spiced soup. Add corn bread and get ready for the Friday field day announcement, "Now, clean sweep down. Sweep all ladders and passageways. Sweep for and aft. Sweep all compartments." Actually, that is a surface ship thing.

TOM HOPELY'S NAVY BEAN SOUP (P-23)

Tom Hopely qualified on the Diablo (SS-479). He was discharged as a second class engineman, then came back in and eventually put in 26 years, retiring as E-6. He says the following about his special Navy Bean Recipe:

"Being a submarine engineman and having been only a mess cook this is the only Navy recipe I have. But bean soup, being one of my favorites, is a blend of the Standard Navy Recipe and one I found in Better Homes and Gardens. I have blended them to my own taste. I took a bowl of it to my American Legion Post 115 pot luck in Beverly, New Jersey and they all thought it was just great. Also I gave a bowl to my 90 year old mother for lunch and she said it was delicious."

Ingredients	Measure/Weight	Method
Beans, Navy, dry	1 pound	
Water	8 cups	
Bone, ham	1	
Ham, diced	1 and 3/4 pound	Bring water to rolling boil. Add beans and cover. Boil for a few minutes and let stand for one hour. Add ham and bone. Recover and simmer for 1 and 1/2 hours until beans are tender.
Carrots, chopped	4 ounces	
Potatoes, diced	2 medium	
Onions, chopped	1 medium	
Thyme	2 tsp	
Old Bay Seafood Seasoning	1 tbsp	Add vegetables and seasoning and continue to simmer. Add water to prevent over reduction.
Tomatoes, canned	1 15 ounce can	

The potatoes eliminate the need for flour. The ham will provide the salt flavor. This is one of those soups that taste good on the first day and even better on the second day.

CHAPTER 23
THE MENU

The submarine menu held a special place in the society of a submarine. Crew members passed the crew's mess while going on watch to check what the day's offerings might include. It was a pleasant task and one that was particularly rewarding in that other crew members were likely to ask, "What's for chow?"

The menu occupied a great deal of the cook's time. It was the basic document that reflected originality, artistry, and culinary competence. It was arranged to provide variety and attraction. It was constrained by several factors the most obvious of which was the availability of food. Other constraints were more subtle. For one thing the commissary officer must approve the menu, the captain must approve the menu and the chief of the boat made demands in the name of the crew.

When asked in the SRC survey if the captain had much influence on the menu, submarine cooks responded in overwhelming negatives. Apparently, most captains believed that what was good for the crew was good for the captain and other officers. Captains were likely to express their opinions about the menu in terms of their likes rather than their dislikes. One captain liked hot bread, another hand whipped chocolate ice cream and still another turtle soup. A few detested liver, onions, turnips, parsnips, Brussels sprouts and a variety of other vegetables.

A captain's dislikes were normally carried to the cook through the commissary officer or executive officer. Sometimes, a captain was only concerned with prohibiting the offending food only in the wardroom. This left the cook freedom to construct a menu reflecting the desires of the crew, while the captain's constraints fell onto the shoulders of the stewards.

An example of a captain's prerogative was submitted by Lieutenant R. E. Shirley to "Dolphin Tales", 1971, edited by Marriete W. Irwin and Julie A. Joa

"The crew of the USS Irex knew that they were going to spend Easter weekend at sea. In order to make the weekend away from their families a little easier, they had planned for joint lay services and an all-hands Easter egg hunt. Among the planners was one who could always be counted on for the unexpected. Ensign Tom Rearer, known as the oldest ensign in the Navy, and maybe the world, since he had previously been CWO2 Tom Rearer, had done a little Easter planning of his own. Tom had carefully noted all the items such as fruit cocktail, sardines, Jello and so forth, which the commanding officer, CDR Robert Koeler, particularly disliked and in fact had banned from the wardroom table, which surely is within the captain's prerogative.

"On Easter morning when Captain Koeler entered the wardroom for breakfast he found, much to his surprise, an Easter basket on his plate. When he opened the basket he was even more surprised to find a chocolate lamb surrounded by colored eggs and some of his more favorite things such as fruit cocktail, Jello and sardines. His curiosity as to whom

was responsible for the deed was quickly satisfied when he read the attached card on which was written, 'Although you may not think this is funny,
Who could get mad at the Easter bunny?'"

One submarine cook, in responding to the survey said that he could write a book about the impositions the commissary officer had on the whole food service operation. Most commissary officers were concerned with balancing the books and that meant he kept an eye on the record keeping. This translated to limiting waste and watching the cost control. He was also likely to watch the timeliness of meal service as well as the cleanliness of the mess and galley. The basic concern for the commissary officer was the same for the captain and cooks themselves: keep the crew happy. Most commissary officers were inclined to let the cooks do their job with as little interference as possible, but there were always exceptions. Take the case of the USS Tinosa (SS-283).

In 1952 Tinosa was ported in San Diego and most of the time operated on a weekly basis. The captain liked to come aboard early on Mondays before going to sea so that he could enjoy the ship's eggs over easy, hash browns, bacon and coffee. This was a ritual with him and everyone knew it.

Carroll W. Davidson, first class cook, dropped from the escape trunk down into the forward torpedo room after a relaxing weekend. He stepped through the hatch into the forward battery and when he passed the wardroom, an arm reached out and grabbed him. The captain pulled him into the small space and pointed to a plate of wieners and sauerkraut in front of him. "What in hell do you call this, Davidson?" the captain demanded.

The cook glanced at the commissary officer who shrunk into a corner of the wardroom. "I don't know captain, but I'll get you your eggs right away," stammered the first class cook. He ran back to the galley where the second class cook, Charles Purung was serving eggs to order to the crew. While continuing to cook eggs to order for the men in the after battery he told Davidson that the commissary officer, who was known to the crew as "Junior" in reference to his stature, had demanded that Purung prepare something special for the captain. Accordingly, the cook had thought that wieners and sauerkraut ought to fill the bill.

Davidson scooped some hash browns and eggs-over-easy onto a plate and carried it quickly to the wardroom. He held the plate as again the captain demanded an explanation. Davidson said that Purung had just followed orders from the commissary officer. The captain's fist banged down on the table so hard the plate of wieners and kraut flipped onto its back. The captain fingered the contents back onto the plate and shoved it over to the commissary officer who ate the 'special breakfast' under the glare of his captain.

The moral of Davidson's story is that it was always a good idea for the commissary officer to stay on the good side of his cooks.

The doctor or pharmacist's mate (corpsman, hospitalman, or M.D.) exercised marginal influence over the menu in terms of nutrition. The menu would have to have been severely lacking for the medical representative to have registered a complaint. For the most part the nutritional aspect of food service was treated so thoroughly in training schools that cooks were not likely to let such an important consideration slide.

The relationship between stewards and cooks was nearly always good for the simple reason that they needed each other. Keeping the wardroom (and therefore the captain) happy was a split responsibility of the two rates. The food had to be good and it had to be served correctly. Some stewards tried to garner the best cuts of meat for the wardroom such as the breast of a chicken, but for the most part the wardroom ate exactly what the crew ate. The stewards would get very nervous if food preparation was late. They put what pressure they could on the cooks who were already sweating it out trying to keep up with the watch schedule. Often, stewards prepared their own meals in their tiny pantry. With hot plate they cooked rice, fish and curry or whatever regional dish attracted them.

Stewards had no input into menu planning, but often conveyed to the cooks the likes and dislikes of the officers. They worked as a team and it was the smart cooks who cut the stewards a little slack in terms of getting the food to the forward battery as quickly as possible.

A comparison of a menu from 1944 and an equivalent menu from 1999 illustrates the development of variety and nutrition in submarine food service.

BREAKFAST

1944	1999
Fresh milk	Eggs to order
Fresh fruit	Hot oatmeal
Creamed minced beef	Waffles
Home fried potatoes	Grilled bacon
Toast	Golden hash browns
B.B.C.	Assorted cereal

NOON MEAL

1944	1999
Creamed veal	Chicken rice soup
Potatoes	El Rancho Beef Stew

Buttered green beans
Celery sticks
Iced vanilla cake
Fresh milk
B.B.C.

Caribbean flounder
Steamed Rice
Buttered pasta
Cauliflower au gratin
Tartar sauce
Baking powder biscuits
Sugar cookies

EVENING MEAL

Rare roast rib of beef
Natural gravy
Cream whipped potatoes
Buttered corn
Fresh milk
Ice cream
B.B.C.

Cream of broccoli soup
Shrimp Jambalaya
Yankee pot roast
Coleslaw
Steamed mixed vegetables
Hot garlic bread
Peanut butter cookies

The USS Segundo menu on the left was a normal menu for the time. The bread, butter and condiments were abbreviated.

Both menus were in-port meals where fresh items were easily procured.

The 1999 menu was that of the USS Pasadena. It named its crew's mess the Rose Bowl Cafe. It presented its menus for a month in advance. The Pasadena menu contained calorie and fat intake for each item per serving. The variety of foods and inclusion of both soup and salad (not listed) were functions of a modified cafeteria style food service. Selection of food using this method was faster. The main dish could be served by mess cooks or cooks from the galley serving-window or placed on serving platters at the tables.

At Christmas and Thanksgiving the red carpet treatment was extended to all hands. In 1962 the USS Tunny Christmas dinner called for a special menu listing the crew, the food and since the boat was ported in Pearl, the salutation, "Mele Kalikimaka". The menu was extravagant even at sea:

> V-8 Cocktail or shrimp cocktail
> Cream of tomato soup
> Baked Hawaiian ham with pineapple sauce and pineapple rings
> Roast young tom turkey with giblet gravy and bread dressing
> Candied sweet potatoes
> Mashed potatoes
> Buttered broccoli
> Creamed peas
> Celery stalks
> Cucumber slices
> Waldorf salad

Combination salad
Fruit cake
Pumpkin pie
Shelled nuts
Hard candy
Ice cream
Brown and serve rolls
Coffee
Butter
Milk

It would be hard to imagine a menu more handsomely constructed than the Tunny 1962 Christmas dinner menu. It is similarly difficult to imagine the huge amount of preparation needed to serve such a variety of food at one meal. Cooks were appreciated at these high times and they deserved the praise. This meal had to prepared in a space about five feet by nine feet, most of which was taken by equipment.

CHAPTER 24
FAVORITE DESSERTS

Submariners always looked forward to dessert. No noon or evening meal was complete without a dessert of some sort. During the Second World War the soft ice cream machine had not yet been invented and so submarine cooks relied heavily on puddings (bread, rice, chocolate, vanilla) and cakes. The ice cream machines were installed on some Guppy submarines during the Cold War and space was allocated for them as nuclear boats came off the ways.

Today, American submarines rely upon the cafeteria serving system for fast meal serving. Submariners choose from a variety of desserts and with attention on calorie intake many low fat desserts are to be found in the chill trays.

The Standard Navy Recipe Service of the 1950s and 60s presented a huge variety of desserts from glazed fruits, fruit pies and fruit cobblers to cakes of every flavor. Pastries have been a traditional baking product since the Second World War. The crews expected their cooks to put out pastries, bread, cakes and cookies. These products in port were most often purchased, but when at sea the cook earned his pay by putting in long hours at the oven.

Coffee cake was often prepared for breakfast and as such could be thought of as a part of the meal rather than a dessert. This section presents a coffee cake recipe with two alternatives for toppings. Most men preferred the dry, crumbly topping that seemed to go so well with early morning hot coffee.

The art of pie crust making was developed by on-the-job training. An apprentice watched a cook/baker work the dough into thin crusts and he duplicated the effort. The recipe is contained herein, but that's just the start.

The filling for pies was usually from a can. Cherry, pumpkin and apple pies had fillings that were partially pre-made. Pies were labor-intensive on submarines just as they are in family kitchens. For that reason the crews were appreciative of the effort and were quick to praise the cooks' work.

When in port baked apples were a favorite dessert. Fresh apples had a fairly long shelf life, but were bulky. They were available mostly for weekly operations and when in port, baked apples were at the top of submariners' favorite desserts.

JIM THOMPSON'S COFFEE CAKE WITH STREUSEL TOPPING, (C-29)

Jim is basically a nuclear type cook. He served on a series of nuclear powered submarines including Thomas Jefferson (SSBN-618), the James K. Polk (SSBN-645), the Robert E. Lee (SSBN-601) and the Archerfish (SSN-678). Then he served on Hardhead (SS-365). He tells briefly of his experience with recipes, "Of course, I went on the boats in 1963. By then, we all got spoiled on all the cake and sweet dough mixes. This was the first time that I had ever used this recipe and I must say it certainly got all the gears turning in my head."

Ingredients	Measure/Weight	Method
Yeast, powder	one package (3/4 oz)	
Water, warm	1/2 cup	About 100 Deg F.
Sugar	1/2 tsp	Combine yeast, warm water and sugar. Stir to dissolve. Then stir again in five minutes. Let stand a total of 10 minutes.
Milk, nonfat, dry	1 tbsp	
Sugar	2 tbsp	
Salt	1/2 tsp	
Mace	pinch	Mix milk, sugar, salt and mace in a mixing bowl.
Shortening	1/2 cup	
Vanilla	1/8 tsp	Add shortening and vanilla. Cream and smooth.
Eggs, room temp.	1 egg	Add egg, flour, water and yeast liquid. Mix until flour is thoroughly moistened. Mix by hand until dough is smooth and elastic. Approximately 10 minutes. Add flour if needed by the teaspoon, only until it begins to pull away from the bowl. Let rise in bowl one hour or until almost double in bulk. Transfer dough to board and kneed. Let rest for 15 minutes. Transfer to greased baking pan. Press dough into baking pan. Score with fork.
Water	1/2 cup	
Flour, white	2 cups	
Egg wash	1 egg, beaten	
Milk	1/2 cup	Mix well in measuring cup or small bowl.

Brush dough in pan with egg wash then sprinkle heavily with Streusel topping. Bake at 425 Deg F for 10 to 15 minutes.

This will make a wonderfully light coffee cake that is perfect for a lingering Sunday morning. Submariners can imagine such a luxurious time in the after battery when the boat lay in relaxed state alongside the tender or pier and the work of the submarine was at a minimum.

JIM THOMPSON'S STREUSEL TOPPING

AND CINNAMON SUGAR MIX

These two toppings are to accompany the coffee cake recipe. Jim speaks of the basic recipe and the toppings:

"The egg wash referred to in the recipe is one that I used while I was on submarines. It can be used on any pastry that requires it, mainly on all pies having a top crust, fruit bars etc. Over the years, I have found this to be a good breakdown.

"Both the Streusel Topping and the Cinnamon Sugar Mix I pulled out of my head, but the coffee cake is from the Standard Navy Recipe. I baked the coffee cake twice, in order to refine the amounts."

STREUSEL TOPPING

Ingredients	Measure/Weight	Method
Butter or margarine	3 tbsp	
Flour	2 tbsp	
Sugar, brown	2 tbsp	
Cinnamon	1 tbsp	
Oats	2 tbsp	Mix by hand until slightly mixed. It should resemble course corn meal.

CINNAMON SUGAR MIX
(an alternate topping)

Ingredients	Measure/Weight	Method
Sugar, powdered	3 tbsp	
Cinnamon	2 tbsp	
Butter, margarine	2 tbsp	Mix by hand until slightly mixed. It should be a crumbled, dry mixture.

CHARLES BROWN'S PIE CRUST (K-1)

The recipe for pie crust contained on this page is the basic Navy recipe for pie crust. It can be used for any of the pie recipes in this publication. The recipe is surprisingly simple and takes a lot less work than one would imagine. In a day when frozen, ready-to-bake pie crusts can be purchased at the local market, amateur cooks are reluctant to try the daunting experience. Let Charles show you how.

Ingredients	Measure/Weight	Method
Flour, all purpose	1 and 1/2 cups	Sift the flour onto waxed paper.
Salt	1/2 tsp	
Baking powder	1 tsp	Mix the dry ingredients and place on a cool mixing board.
Shortening	3 tbsp	Start with one half the dry mixture. Add all of the shortening/butter. Work the mixture by hand until it is smooth. Add the remaining dry ingredients and again mix by hand.
Butter	3 tbsp	
Water, iced	1/4 cup	Add the ice water and continue to mix until the dough becomes a ball. Remove from bowl and place on board. Knead the dough until it is smooth. Roll the dough to a two inch thickness. Divide the dough in half. Continue to roll each half into thin fourteen inch circles. Place in nine inch pie pans, crimp edges, trim and bake at 450 Deg F until crusts are a light brown.

Add the pie contents and continue to bake as prescribed. If a top crust is desired double the recipe quantities. This recipe takes a bit of practice and a bit of work, but it's worth it because the mark of a true culinary artist is his ability to turn out great pies from scratch.

SAM PALMER'S CHERRY PIE (K-18)

Chapter 17 has the story of Commissaryman Greenwood, a fictitious character who trusted the Acme Pie Company to deliver to the Razorback in San Diego savory cherry pies. It was his undoing, because the crew was unable to find cherries in Acme's cherry pies. Sam and Betty Palmer guarantee that the recipe for their cherry pie has lots of cherries. The recipe was taken from the 1963 Standard Navy Recipe Service. Sam qualified in 1949 and served aboard several diesel and nuclear powered submarines. He is a Holland Club member.

Ingredients	Measure/Weight	Method
Cherries, red, sour	28 ounce can	Drain cherries into bowl and set aside. Add enough water to cherry juice to make 3/4 pint. Heat about half of the cherry juice to boiling point. Mix cornstarch with remainder of cold cherry juice and stir mixture into warmed cherry juice above. Cook and stir constantly until thickened. Add sugar and bring mixture to a boil, stirring constantly until the sugar is completely dissolved. Remove from heat and blend in food color and lemon juice. Carefully fold in the drained cherries. Allow filling to cool. Pour filling into pie shells. Bake pies at 425 deg F for 30 minutes or until crust is brown.
Cherry juice	3/4 pint	
Cornstarch	4 tbsp	
Sugar, granulated	1 cup	
Salt	pinch	
Lemon juice	1 tsp	
Food coloring	dash	
Pie shells, 9 inch	2	

Sam and Betty Palmer have grand children who are always ready for cherry pie. To scale down the pie making process so that fresh-baked pie is available to the kids on demand, the Palmers have a short-cut method. Press into five cereal bowls refrigerated Bisquick or Pillsbury ready-made biscuits, to make pie shells. Scale down the Navy recipe to one small can of cherries, 8 ounces of water/juice mix, 2 ounces of corn starch, six ounces of sugar, a pinch of salt and a few drops of lemon juice. Follow the Navy instructions and scoop the prepared mix into the biscuit-lined bowls. Bake the mini-pies in the oven at about 375 deg F for about 15 minutes or until the shells are brown and the cherry mix is bubbling.

An alternate for the grand kids is to combine the mini-cherry mix with muffin mix where the muffin acts as the base crust. Cinnamon bun mix can be used by slicing them into strips and criss-crossing the cherry filled muffins with a top-crust.

According to the Palmers the cook needs to stand back as the kids go for the cherry mini-pies in a big way.

GEORGE LEVITT'S PUMPKIN PIE (K-34)

George Levitt qualified on the Dace (SS-247) and served his submarine career entirely on that boat. He was a radar technician second class on the Dace back in the days when radar on the boats was something new.

Here is a great pumpkin pie recipe that is from the Standard Navy Recipe Service. The wonderful aroma of spices that filled the boats from baking pumpkin pies is fondly remembered by many submariners that participated in this study. When the pies were set out on the crew's mess tables to cool a mess cook had to keep watch over them. Even the torpedomen in the after room came forward to smell the pies and drool.

Ingredients	Measure/Weight	Method
Sugar	2/3 cup	
Salt	1/2 tsp	
Flour	1/8 cup	
Cinnamon, ground	1 and 1/2 tsp	
Nutmeg, ground	1/2 tsp	
Ginger, ground	1/2 tsp	
Pumpkin, canned	1 can, 15 oz.	
Milk, whole	1 and 1/2 cups	
Eggs	2 large	Mix together the sugar, salt, flour, cinnamon, nutmeg and ginger. Blend in the pumpkin. Add milk and again blend into a smooth mixture. Let stand for one hour. Add eggs, mixing in thoroughly. Pour into previously baked pie crust. Bake at 375 DegF for 45 minutes. Test for doneness by inserting toothpick and check it for dryness.

George offers his own pie crust instructions. This uses an electric beater.

The pie crust is made as follows: Sift 2 cups of flour into a bowl. Add 2/3 cup shortening and blend by hand. Mix at slow speed for about 1/2 minute. Dissolve 1 tbsp salt into 5 tbsp water and add this slowly to the flour mixture while continuing on low speed. When mixture has turned to dough place in refrigerator for about one hour. Sprinkle dough, board, rolling pin with flour and roll dough flat, 1/8 inch thick. Press into pie tin and prick holes in bottom. Trim sides. Bake crust at 450 DegF for ten minutes until golden brown.

CHARLES BROWN'S SWEET POTATO AND PUMPKIN PIE

The longer a cook served in submarines and learned his trade the more the crew and captain learned to trust the ship's cook. This trust invited the cook to move away from the Standard Navy Recipes and to become a little more creative. Here is Charles Brown's special pie that he served on at least two submarines with great success. It is geared to Thanksgiving and Christmas holidays.

Ingredients	Measure/Weight	Method
Pumpkin, canned	2 and 1/2 cans	
Sweet potatoes, canned	2 and 1/2 cans	Using an electric mixer on low speed, mash and whip the sweet potatoes in a large bowl for two to three minutes. Use the liquid contents of the can to provide a smooth texture.
Salt	1 and 1/2 tsp	
Sugar, brown	2 cups	
Cinnamon, ground	1 and 1/2 tsp	Add the pumpkin to the sweet potato mix. Add the dry ingredients and mix until blended.
Nutmeg, ground	3/4 tsp	
Ginger, ground	3/4 tsp	
Cloves, ground	1/4 tsp	
Eggs	4 large	Add the eggs to the mix and blend until smooth.
Egg nog	1 quart	Add the egg nog and mix until smooth. Transfer the mixture into a large pot and cook while stirring over a low heat until the mixture begins to thicken. Remove from heat. Ladle the thickened mixture into two lightly browned pie crusts. Bake in a pre-heated oven at 450 Deg F until the crust is golden brown and filling is solid. Use a toothpick to test.

Let the pies cool and serve with whipped cream or ice cream. They make a wonderful and different Thanksgiving Day and Christmas dessert.

WARREN HUGHE'S BAKED APPLES (G-19)

This is a Grouper (SS-214) favorite and contributed to the crew's name of Jellybellies. Baked apples could really only be put on the menu when the boat was in port or on weekly operations since fresh apples had to be used. Fresh apples were also to be found in Waldorf salad, but the best apple was fresh and chilled to be eaten where ever the men worked. Never the less, baked apples were real hits for dessert and the last section to eat was lucky to find enough for every man.

Ingredients	Measure/Weight	Method
Apples, baking	4	Pre-heat oven to 375 Deg F. Wash and core apples to about 1/2 inch of bottom. Peel 1 inch strip of skin around middle of each apple or peel upper half.
Sugar, brown	4 tbsp	
Butter	4 tsp	
Cinnamon	1/2 tsp	
Nutmeg	1/8 tsp	Mix ingredients with enough water to make a paste or heavy syrup. Pour or push mixture into hollowed centers and tops of apples. Bake 30 to 40 minutes or until tender when pierced with a fork.

An ice cream topping can provide variety. Baked apples can be microwaved rather than convection oven baked. The recipe is the same and microwave time is about 5 to 10 minutes.

Many variations call for raisins to be mixed into the syrup. A crunchy texture can be obtained by mixing broken gingersnap cookies into the syrup. Chopped nuts provide another texture variation.

HOWARD SMAY'S BREAD PUDDING (G-2)

Howard is a Second World War veteran and qualified on the S-45 in 1939. He made several patrols in S boats and several more in fleet type boats. His first greatest challenge as a successful submarine ship's cook came during the early years of the war when meager and very different provisions were all that was available on the Australian market. A second challenge was the tender-provided food that was weevil infested and stale.

There's just something about bread pudding that is truly American. During the great depression of the thirties stale bread was hoarded in anticipation of bread pudding. Howard Smay is an expert at conversion and he describes the process as follows:

"My many adult grandchildren arrived for a visit. They were captivated by the Submarine Cuisine research project. They implored me to convert the Navy recipe to properly serve our little group. I assured them that it was a simple matter to convert any Navy recipe to serve any size group."

The following serves between three and four people.

Ingredients	Measure/Weight	Method
Bread, dry, toasted	1 and 1/2 slices	Cut bread into inch cubes. Place lightly pieces in an eight inch cake pan.
Eggs	2 eggs, minus 1 yoke	
Sugar	3 tbsp	
Salt	pinch	
Nutmeg	pinch	
Vanilla	1/2 tsp	
Butter	2 and 1/2 tsp	
Milk, scalded	1 and 1/4 cups	Heat the milk to just under boiling. Mix together ingredients. Gradually add hot milk to egg mixture, stirring constantly. Pour egg and milk mixture over bread pieces. Allow to stand for five minutes.
Raisins	1/4 cup	Fold raisins into mixture. Bake at 325 Deg F approximately one hour or until pudding is firm.

Howard also offers the following:

"It's important to soak the bread in the mixture long enough so that it doesn't float when baking.

"Serve the pudding hot or cold. If served hot a dab of Cool Whip brings back memories of whipped Avoset that submariners enjoyed on the old S-45, some sixty years ago. Many restaurants now serve bread pudding with a whiskey sauce."

JOHN FRANKLIN'S CREAMY RICE PUDDING (G-11)

Chief Commissaryman Franklin qualified aboard the Charr (SS-328), then served on the Bugara (SS-331), Sea Dragon (SSN-584) and Tirante (SS-420). He knew the importance of a healthy and filling dessert. The Rice Pudding could be made equally as well from fresh or canned milk or a combination of them. This meant that rice pudding could be served for as long as the eggs held out.

Ingredients	Measure/Weight	Method
Rice	1/2 pound	Bring water to a boil. Add rice and salt. Stir occasionally to free rice from sticking.
Water	1 quart	
Salt	2 tbsp	
Milk	1 quart	Heat milk to just under boiling.
Sugar	6 ounces	Mix dry ingredients thoroughly
Cornstarch	2 tbsp	
Salt	1/2 tsp	
Cinnamon	1/4 tsp	
Nutmeg	1/4 tsp	
Milk	1 cup	Mix the chilled milk with the dry ingredients.
Eggs	3 large	Blend eggs into mixture. Add mixture to hot milk, stirring with wire whisk. Cook for 5 minutes or until thickened, stirring constantly.
Butter, melted	1/4 stick	
Vanilla	1 tsp	Turn off the heat and allow to slightly cool. Add raisin mix. Add rice after draining excess water. Stir mixture thoroughly. Pour into shallow pan. Cover with waxed paper and place in refrigerator. Dust surface with cinnamon and nutmeg.
Raisins	2 cups	

The texture of the rice pudding was delicate and the combination of spices and rice gave a rich flavor. The dessert may be served hot, but submariners invariably wanted it cold in large serving bowls.

GEORGE LEVITT'S VANILLA CREAM PUDDING (G-18)

Vanilla pudding was not only a favorite of the crew in terms of a dessert, it could also become a bed for frozen or canned fruit. The only drawback to the recipe is that it called for fresh milk and this limited the recipe's use to in-port or short transits. The recipe won't work using dehydrated milk, however, cooks reported that it did work using condensed milk although the flavor was altered.

Ingredients	Measure/Weight	Method
Milk, whole	1 qt.	Heat milk to nearly boiling.
Flour, sifted	7/8 cup	
Sugar, granulated	1 cup	Make a paste of flour, sugar, salt and cold milk. Slowly stir the paste into the hot milk. Cook for approximately 10 minutes, stirring frequently.
Salt	1/4 tsp	
Milk, whole	3/8 cup	
Eggs, beaten	2 large	Mix a small amount of the hot cream mixture with the beaten eggs. Add to hot mixture. Cook five minutes longer. Turn off the heat, blend in the vanilla and allow to stand for twenty minutes. Pour into serving dishes.
Vanilla extract	2 tbsp	

This recipe makes six servings. Vanilla pudding can be used in a variety of ways, forming the base for fresh fruit toppings. For example, a biscuit smothered with vanilla pudding and then layered with fresh fruit makes an elegant dessert.

CHAPTER 25
BAKING IN A SUBMARINE

Nothing was so appreciated on a submarine as a fine baker. The art of baking was an integral part of being a submarine cook. On the other hand the two art forms were not necessarily inter-dependent. Some very fine cooks were lousy bakers and in a few instances, good bakers were rotten cooks. Putting out good meals on a daily basis represented the foundation of submarine food service, however, cakes, pastries, pies and cookies turned the competent cook into a true artist. Nothing was so appreciated by a submarine crew as hot biscuits in the morning or fresh sticky buns for the four-to-eight watch. What's more, the aroma of baking in the wee hours of the night wafted its way through the boat and momentarily masked the natural smell of sweat and diesel fuel.

The pressure placed on submarine cooks to bake was only experienced when underway for extended periods. While in port the cooks simply purchased baked goods from vendors. On special occasions the cooks might come to the boat to bake during the night, but these instances were rare and the captain did not expect such devotion to duty. A junior cook was always encouraged to bake while in port, because the skill of baking was important for advancement in rate. Normally, in-port training in baking centered around pies and hot rolls.

Buying prepared food from vendors rather than baking could be done to excess even when the boat was in port. Few crew members had any real appreciation of the time required to bake. They simply expected quality in the baked goods they ate and how the goods appeared in the crew's mess was ordinarily not their concern. When a lead cook cut corners and placed too much trust in vendors there could be complaints. The gripes normally were directed at the cook, but when satisfaction was not forthcoming the crew could find other means of redress. The following happened to Lieutenant Gilhooly, commissary officer in "Of Wives and Submarines":

"An engineman came thumping up the passageway and stopped in front of the wardroom door. He waited for recognition, and Gil looked up from the dispatches to inquire what was up.

"'You might want to be a witness to what's going on in the crew's mess, Mr. Gilhooly.' The petty officer's face was under a deep frown that spelled trouble.

"Gil followed the engineman to the crew's mess where a horde of sailors hovered over ten pies, placed five to a table. Gil said nothing since he could see no blood or anything suggesting violence. He just watched.

"The auxiliaryman who had replaced Gilhooly's metal screws with machine screws brandished a knife. 'Now we'll see just what our cook has been up to!' announced the burly sailor in triumph. He examined the knife with the eye of a surgeon, and satisfied with its edge, carefully removed the crust from each pie. These he stacked on a plate. Then he assigned one crew member to each pie, instructing as follows, 'You guys be careful now. I want a fair and impartial count.' Gilhooly had missed the introductory remarks, and had not a clue as to what this experiment was all about.

"Each man fingered through the gooey red gelatin, removing what cherries could be found in each pie. Gil was astonished to learn that one of the pies had only two cherries in it. The average count, after the mathematics had been done on a red gelatin-spotted sheet of Razorback stationary, stood at 4.6 cherries per pie.

"Just as we thought. The boat is being swindled by the Acme Pastry Company.' These were the fighting words of one Harold Webster, cherry count mathematician, electronics technician and Don Juan extraordinaire. An exceptional man among men of high caliber, he had gained a reputation as Razorback's biggest liberty hound and connoisseur of women. The fact that he had remained on board for this occasion was testimony to the strong feelings of the crew on the subject of Razorback's pastries.

"It was no accident that the decapitation of ten pies had been timed to coincide with Gilhooly's duty day. The erudite Webster stepped to the front of this incensed crowd and addressed the commissary officer in well-chosen words. 'We have gathered here, today, Mr. Gilhooly, to perform a completely unbiased inventory of cherries. By the numbers, which I point out cannot lie, we must conclude that the Acme Pastry Company has systematically engaged in fraud against the men of the Razorback. This disgusting practice has gone on for years while we have complained bitterly to our cook, Mr. Charles Greenwood. And why, do you ask, does our esteemed cook continue to do business with such an underhanded company? Because, Mr. Gilhooly, the delivery boy brings the pies to the boat, shuttles them down the hatch and places them in the cool box. Thus, you can see that Greenwood buys from Acme because he is too lazy to bring the pies into the boat. In short, his liberty is at our expense.'

"The electronics technician bowed and the gloating crew members applauded. Gilhooly was swept up into the righteous indignation of the men gathered on this momentous occasion. He vowed to the men that this abominable situation would not be allowed to continue, and that he would personally take charge of the matter. The men cheered and were the spectacle not to have been inside a submarine, Mr. Gilhooly would have been carried to his quarters on the shoulders of the men. As it was, he simply retired back to the forward battery to drink his now cold cup of coffee."

A submarine's lead cook was under the scrutiny of the crew when at sea and when in port. The crew didn't care about how he might juggle the books, but if they suspected him of cutting corners just to cut himself a little slack they were likely to object bitterly.

When the boat was underway both the captain and crew greatly desired all kinds of fresh baked goods. The most popular and often baked goods included corn bread, biscuits, cakes, doughnuts, cookies, pies, and pizza. Other foods such as puddings and fruit bars were baked. It is interesting that bread was baked after the normal vendor-baked bread was consumed. This meant that daily and weekly operations demanded very little from submarine cooks in the way of baking. But when the boat set to sea for a prolonged period either in transit or patrol the cooks became bakers. Of all the baked goods turned out by submarine cooks the quality of fresh baked bread was the litmus test for a true baker.

Stories abound about the conditions of baking during the Second World War. Bread was baked as a matter of course, but invasions of weevils into the flour were a constant problem. Two distinct philosophies have been recorded regarding the weevils. On the one hand some cooks went out of their way to sift the flour and chase down every last little intruder. This produced bread that was pure white and delicious. On the other hand many cooks believed that there were redeeming features to the weevils. After all, they represented nutrients not found in pristine flour. These cooks produced bread that had a remarkable similarity to raisin bread. Crew members were divided as to those who held each slice of bread to the light and meticulously picked out the dead weevils before eating it and those older salts who believed that the crunchiness was a welcome addition to the bread's texture.

Only the smell of fresh baked bread surpassed the aroma of hot buns. Quality bread and other baked goods while at sea played a direct and strong role in the positive morale of the crew. The men's birthdays were often celebrated with a birthday cake complete with frosting and candles. A good chief of the boat could spot the home-sickness in some of the young crew members and he would often get the word to the cooks in time for a small recognition of the youngster as a valued crew member. It was this kind of thoughtfulness that turned a collection of sailors into a crew. The central figure was the submarine cook performing his duties as ship's baker.

CHAPTER 26
PATROL REPORTS

The Medical Department of the Submarine Base at New London conducted a habitability survey of about 1200 patrol reports, mostly from the Second World War. The conclusions of this survey corroborate the information found elsewhere in this publication. If the findings could be summarized they would include the following regarding the limitations of food service on fleet type and Guppy submarines.

    1. Space limitations in submarines preclude the storage of adequate food for the types and length of patrols required in global confrontations.

    2. Even though food preservation techniques have improved during the period of the Second World War and Korean Conflict submarines are severely limited in their ability to carry the food bulk necessary for prolonged periods at sea.

    3. The lack of adequate food storage and preservation in submarines produces crew ailments including, gum deterioration, loss of teeth, debilitating anemia and lethargy.

    4. Many of the crew ailments can be forestalled by the use of vitamin and mineral tables taken on a daily basis. The greatest hazard to good health of crew members is the lack of vitamin C and the lack of fresh vegetables and fruits.

Blenny (SS-324) made a WesPac cruise in 1952. During the six month deployment the boat made 177 dives, spent 991 hours submerged, and traveled 21,000 miles. During the deployment the boat's officers and crew consumed 36.5 tons of food and 2,912 gallons of coffee.

The following is a segment of the 1953 patrol report for the USS Blackfin (SS-322) after its return to the home port after a 56 day patrol during the Cold War.

Health - In general, the state of health was good. During the first two weeks at sea colds increased slightly. One case of influenza, virus unknown and one case of acute laryngitis were treated. No man-days were lost to sickness.

Food - The ship was provisioned as follows:
Fresh vegetables and fruit	3 weeks
Frozen vegetables	8 weeks
Fresh potatoes	5 weeks
Dry stores	12 weeks
Meat	8 weeks
Preserved meats	12 weeks

On this cruise, 1500 pounds of bread mix, 600 pounds of flour, and 800 pounds of soup barely lasted eight weeks. Large quantities of snacks were consumed.

Prefabricated meat and fowl, powdered milk and cream and premixed bakery items were provisions worthy of note. Milk was served at breakfast throughout the entire patrol.

Approximately 1500 Hexa-Vitamin tablets were dispensed.

Through inexperience canned sugar and coffee were stowed in the engine rooms. Some of this was contaminated with fuel oil when the cans "breathed" through their "press-on" lids while snorkeling.

The report speaks of condensation, air revitalization through snorkeling and the excellent protection provided by exposure suits in the northern reaches. Most of us would take exception to this latter claim but the references to food and vitamins are in accordance with the findings of the New London Medical Team.

It may be worthwhile to conclude this analysis with a memory of one who was there, a submarine cook, Frank Payeur of Dogfish, Sablefish and Sea Owl.

"We had to be pretty innovative with our hamburger - Shepherd's Pie, Chili, Tacos, Pasta Sauce and Stuffed Peppers.

"Avoset was a sterilized cream fortified with vitamin D and it was issued to supplement our lack of sunshine. It made a wonderful addition to mashed potatoes, cream sauces, white sauces and an addition to powdered milk. It even made into a whipped cream of sorts."

Food was often relegated to a secondary consideration by submarine designers, but this information suggests that food in submarines may be the most critical factor in submarine deployment.

Nuclear powered submarines provide for sanitation, exercise and adequate sleeping. The fast attack type nuclear submarine does not provide a great improvement on the earlier diesel powered submarine relative to food storage capacity. The Trident type submarine represents a huge leap forward by virtue of its size and design.

As the Virginia class submarine design accommodates better food storage and preservation system the question arises as to the limiting factor of patrol endurance. At this point in time the limitations of food storage may be surpassed by the psychological limitations of long patrols away from home and with only limited access to the outside world.

NOTES

The single most important factor affecting the morale of submarine sailors is the quality of the food they eat. From the captain to the lowliest seaman each member of a submarine crew expects and deserves the very best of the Navy's culinary arts – and that's exactly what they get, the very best. Now you can duplicate these recipes in your kitchen and can bring back the taste of submarine cuisine.

This publication contains:

- Favorite dishes of submariners – special sauces, drawing out the natural flavors, preparing exotic desserts.

- Recipes geared to your kitchen so you can duplicate the greatest meals served from the Second World War to America's latest submarine, the USS Virginia.

- Secrets of food preparation that turn ordinary commodities into delicious culinary delights.

- Descriptions of what it takes to be an American submarine cook, of how these great chefs overcome the problem of cramped quarters and how they cater to the demands of discriminating submariners.

Printed in Great Britain
by Amazon